DOGFIGHT 6

Me 262
Northwest Europe 1944–45

Robert Forsyth

OSPREY PUBLISHING
Bloomsbury Publishing Plc
Kemp House, Chawley Park, Cumnor Hill, Oxford,
OX2 9PH, UK
29 Earlsfort Terrace, Dublin 2, Ireland
1385 Broadway, 5th Floor, New York, NY 10018, USA
E-mail; info@ospreypublishing.com
www.ospreypublishing.com

OSPREY is a trademark of Osprey Publishing Ltd

First published in Great Britain in 2023

A catalogue record for this book is available from the British
Library.

ISBN: PB 9781472850515; eBook 9781472850522;
ePDF 9781472850539; XML 9781472850546

23 24 25 26 27   10 9 8 7 6 5 4 3 2 1

Edited by Tony Holmes
Cover and battlescene artwork by Gareth Hector
Ribbon and tactical diagrams by Tim Brown
Armament artwork by Jim Laurier
Maps by www.bounford.com
Index by Fionbar Lyons
Typeset by PDQ Digital Media Solutions, UK
Printed and bound in India by Replika Press Private Ltd.

Osprey Publishing supports the Woodland Trust, the UK's
leading woodland conservation charity.

To find out more about our authors and books visit
www.ospreypublishing.com. Here you will find extracts, author
interviews, details of forthcoming events and the option to sign
up for our newsletter.

Front Cover Artwork: On 10 April 1945, 1,232 B-17s and
B-24s of the USAAF's Eighth Air Force, bringing nearly 900
escort fighters with them, targeted German airfields, transport
hubs and a military infrastructure centre at Oranienburg,
Rechlin, Neuruppin, Stendal, Brandenburg-Briest, Zerbst,
Burg, Parchim and Wittenberge. The respective *Staffeln* of JG 7
had been placed at readiness during the morning, and the
German raid reporting system began plotting the incursion
sometime after midday. Oberleutnant Walter Schuck, leading
seven Me 262s of 3./JG 7 in his 'Yellow 1' to intercept,
achieved the impressive distinction of shooting down four
B-17s within eight minutes over Oranienburg between 1430
and 1438 hrs for his 203rd to 206th victories. Gareth Hector
depicts the moment when Schuck passed above his second
victim, B-17G 44-8427 *HENN'S REVENGE*, flown by
2Lt Robert I. Murray, of the 358th BS/303rd BG. The USAAF
reported that the 'Missing aircraft held course for very few
seconds after being hit, then peeled slightly up and then slid
over and down to the right through [the] formation. Appeared
to be out of control'. The shooting down of *HENN'S
REVENGE* marked Schuck's 204th aerial victory.

Previous Page: As the Allies advanced across Germany in the
spring of 1945, capturing airfields which lay in their paths, so
they discovered abandoned Me 262s, many in a relatively intact
condition. This example, adorned with the emblem of JG 7, is
Wk-Nr. 112385 'Yellow 8' of 3. *Staffel*, which was found at
Stendal. It had suffered Flak damage after being hit by fire from
an overzealous German airfield gun battery. (EN Archive)

Acknowledgements – Firstly, I would like to acknowledge the
former Me 262 pilots whom I met and with whom I
corresponded in the late 1980s and early 1990s: Hermann
Buchner, Adolf Galland, Walter Hagenah, Erich Hohagen,
Walter Krupinski, Klaus Neumann, Eduard Schallmoser and
Walter Windisch, whose collective recollections are used in this
book. I must also mention Willi Unger who recalled what it
was like to fly piston-engined fighters against the USAAF's
raids. My thanks also to the following former USAAF personnel
who were kind enough to give me their recollections of
encountering and combating the Me 262: Oliven T. Cowan,
James J. Finnegan, John O. Moench, William P. Morton, Jonny
Quong, Robert M. Radlein, James L. Stalter and James L.
Vining. Over the years I have been very grateful for assistance
and contributions from Nevill Basnett, Nick Beale, Walter
Boyne, Stephen Chapis, Eddie Creek, John M. Gray, Manfred
Griehl, Tony Holmes, Lorenz Rasse, Rudolf Schallmoser and
J. Richard Smith. Finally, my thanks to Tony Holmes for the
concept and the brief, and to Gareth Hector, Tim Brown and
Jim Laurier for bringing the book 'alive' with their excellent
artwork and graphics.

Contents

CHAPTER 1
IN BATTLE

In the early morning of 10 April 1945, airfields across the east of England reverberated to the thunder of more than 6,000 aero engines. The USAAF's Eighth Air Force was once more assembling a massive force to bomb targets in Germany. This time, no fewer than 1,315 B-17 Flying Fortresses and B-24 Liberators would strike at a range of airfields including Oranienburg, Brandenburg-Briest, Parchim, Burg-bei-Magdeburg and Rechlin-Lärz, known to be used by the Me 262 jet fighters of *Jagdgeschwader* (JG) 7, which defended northern Germany and the approach to Berlin. The bombers would also target a main ammunition storage depot and regional rail yards, and they would be escorted by 905 fighters, most of them P-51 Mustangs, but also a force of 62 P-47 Thunderbolts.

As the morning progressed, the huge American formation crossed the English coast south of Lowestoft, in Suffolk, and headed across the North Sea and over the Zuider Zee on its course into what remained of the Third Reich. By early afternoon the bombers were heading northwest between Bremen and Hannover. From midday, as they penetrated ever deeper into German airspace, they were tracked by the Luftwaffe's raid reporting network which fed information to the *Staffeln* of JG 7 waiting to intercept. Indeed, this day would see a major commitment launched by the *Geschwader*'s dwindling number of jets against the bombers, although it could be argued that the defenders had left things until too late.

At Burg airfield, the bombing was to prove catastrophic for the German units based there. Hangars and workshops were either destroyed or badly damaged, and at least 200 bombs fell on the runways and taxi-tracks. Many aircraft were also destroyed, including a number of Bf 109/Ju 88 *Mistel* combinations needed for operations against the bridges over the Oder which were under threat from the Soviets.

Just after 1400 hrs, as the Americans pulled away from Burg, Me 262s from III./JG 7 took off from Parchim in pouring rain that reduced visibility down to 2,000m. As they did so, P-51s fell onto the vulnerable jets whilst they climbed

into the sky, shooting down at least two. Thirty minutes later, the bombs from the B-24s of the 2nd Air Division fell on Parchim, narrowly missing the airfield itself to fall on open ground, although some buildings and personnel were killed in the attack.

As this was happening, more Me 262s took off from Oranienburg, Rechlin-Lärz and Brandenburg-Briest, having been directed to take on the bombers of the 1st Air Division which the German fighter controllers thought – wrongly – were heading for Berlin.

Among their pilots was Leutnant Walter Hagenah of 9./JG 7, whose home city of Bremen, 250km away to the west, had suffered its fair share of bombing. He knew this because before training on the Me 262, from the late summer of 1944 he had flown as a *Sturmgruppe* pilot with IV.(*Sturm*)/JG 3, undertaking close-range attacks against bombers over northwest Germany in heavily armed and armoured Fw 190s. Because of his experience in more than 100 air combat missions, his success in claiming in excess of ten aerial victories and as a *Sturmjäger*, Hagenah had been reassigned to 2./*Jagdgruppe Nord* at Sagan-Küpper under Oberleutnant Georg Radel in November.

There, Hagenah was involved in converting former bomber pilots – by that time, largely redundant – to flying the Fw 190 fighter for missions in defence of the Reich. Subsequently, when his *Staffel* was redesignated 2. *Ergänzungsjagdgeschwader* (EJG) 1 at Lüben, as its commander he oversaw the training up of new pilots for the *Sturmgruppen*. But in late February 1945 Hagenah was reassigned again to commence some very rudimentary and hurried

The daunting sight of a formation of B-17G Flying Fortresses from the 532nd and 535th BSs of the 381st BG, based at Ridgewell, in Essex. Such formations could spread across miles of sky and number many hundreds of bombers, with each aircraft armed with as many as 13 Browning M2 0.50-cal. machine guns. Approaching such an 'armada' was therefore challenging, even for an aircraft as fast as the Me 262. (Author's Collection)

Opposing the USAAF raid of 10 April 1945 were the Me 262A-1as of JG 7, two of which are seen here at Brandenburg-Briest in February of that year. The aircraft at right carries the fuselage markings of the *Geschwaderkommodore*, Major Theodor Weissenberger, and also has the tactical number green '4' applied just below the *Geschwader* emblem on the nose. The aircraft to left also bears the chevron of a *Stab* machine. (EN Archive)

training for the Me 262, after which he joined III./JG 7 at Parchim in March. He recounted:

> The *Gruppe* had just moved from Parchim to Lärz, and although we had a full establishment of 30 aircraft, only about half of them were serviceable. Enemy bombers had been observed moving in to attack Berlin and my unit was one of those ordered to engage them. But during start-up, my right engine refused to light and I had to stay behind. It took the technicians about 15 minutes to get the engine running, and then, with another Me 262 flown by a young Feldwebel, I took off late to engage the bombers.
>
> We received no instructions from the ground when airborne – our task was merely to 'engage bombers over Berlin'. Once above cloud at about 5,000m, I could see the bomber formation clearly at about 6,000m. I was flying at about 550km/h in a slight climb after them. Everything seemed to be going fine; in three to four minutes we would be with the bombers. Then, as an experienced fighter pilot, I had the old 'tingling at the back of the neck' feeling that perhaps enemy fighters were about.
>
> I had a good look around, and in front and above I saw six Mustangs passing above me from almost head-on. At first I thought they had not seen me, and so I continued on. But, just to be on the safe side, I glanced back once more – and it was a good thing for me that I did, because at that moment, I saw the Mustangs diving down and curving round onto the pair of us. With the speed of their dive, and the speed we had lost because of our climb, they stood a good chance of catching us. Then they opened fire and tracer began to flash disconcertingly close to our aircraft. I opened my throttle fully and put my nose down a little to increase my own speed, and resolved to outrun the enemy fighters. I did not attempt to throw off their aim – I knew the moment I turned my speed would fall, and then they would have me. I told the Feldwebel on my left to keep going, but obviously he became scared because I noticed him weaving from side to side, then he turned away to the left.
>
> It was just what the Mustang pilots wanted, and in no time they had broken off from me and were onto him. His aircraft received several hits and I saw it go down and crash; my companion was unable to bail out. I kept an eye on the enemy fighters at 4,000m and watched them reform and turn round to fly westwards for home. Feeling vengeful, I decided to have a go at them.
>
> I rapidly closed in on them from behind, but at a range of about 500m the Mustang leader started rocking his wings and I knew I had been seen. If I continued I knew that the enemy fighters would probably split up into two and curve round from either side onto my tail, so I resolved to strike first. I loosed off all 24 of the R4M rockets under my wings straight at the enemy fighters, and I was very lucky; I hit two of them and they went down out of control. This time I had plenty

of speed, and had little trouble in avoiding the fire from their companions. But I had no time for self-congratulation, because my own fuel was beginning to run short and I had to get down as soon as I could.

I picked up a beacon on my receiver and found that it was the airfield at Köthen. I called up the airfield on the radio and I said I wanted to land there, but they called back and warned me to be careful as there were *Indiana* [enemy fighters] over the field. When I arrived, I saw that there were enemy fighters about trying to strafe the field, but the light Flak defences were giving them a hard time and I managed to slip in unnoticed. Suddenly, however, it seems I *was* noticed, because almost as one, the Mustangs packed up and went home; perhaps they thought my own and other jet fighters had come to tackle them. Certainly they did not know I was short of fuel. I made a tight, curving approach and hurled the Messerschmitt on to the runway, breathing a sigh of relief at having got down safely. But then the Mustangs must have realised what was going on, and in a trice they were back over the airfield and it was my turn to have a rough time. But fortunately for me, the Flak defences were still on their toes and I was not hit.

Leutnant Walter Hagenah of 9./JG 7 was a former *Sturmgruppe* instructor who converted to flying jets. He was credited with the destruction of a P-51 on 10 April 1945, bringing his total victory claims to 17 during the course of 140 missions. (Author's Collection, courtesy of Hagenah)

Meanwhile, Hagenah's comrades in III./JG 7 engaged the B-17s of the 1st Air Division as they reached their targets of Oranienburg and Rechlin. The Eighth Air Force post-mission narrative adds to Hagenah's account in illustrating what these missions were like to fly – for both sides:

The lead and second groups were first hit by a total of about 12 Me 262s which attacked singly and in pairs, pressing their attacks closely and, in some cases, flying right through the formation. Enemy aircraft were very aggressive and daring, attacking from the tail, level and above, closing to within very short distances. From these attacks the 1st Air Division lost five B-17s to enemy aircraft and claimed 7-1-8 [destroyed-probable-damaged] Me 262s. Fighter escort was reported to have done an excellent job of breaking up any formations before they could get through to the bombers.

For the bomber crews, however, even at this late stage of the war, reaching targets as far east as Burg, Parchim, Oranienburg and Brandenburg was no picnic, and the presence of the high-speed Me 262 jet interceptor armed with heavy-calibre cannon and rockets, flown by determined pilots made the job all the harder. Even in April 1945, for the Allied aircrews, nothing could be taken for granted.

CHAPTER 2

SETTING THE SCENE

The arrival of the Me 262 in the skies over northwest Europe in the summer of 1944 was representative of the dichotomy facing the German military at that stage of the war. Messerschmitt's designers and engineers had created a pioneering aircraft, incorporating the most advanced design and aerodynamic refinements, and powered by the jet engine, an innovative and ground-breaking form of propulsion. Professor Willy Messerschmitt's creation was truly a design that would change everything, and quite possibly return the strategic edge to Germany in the war in the air. But the key word here is 'possibly' because, in a trend that dogged the Luftwaffe from mid-1943 onwards, while the design and engineering was there, the manufacturing capability to equip its units *quickly* and in *mass* simply was not.

By May 1944, Germany was engaged in a multi-front war in the Mediterranean, on the Eastern Front and in the defence of the airspace over the homeland against the Allied strategic bomber offensive. As such, the Luftwaffe was slowly being bled dry in terms of pilots and fuel; it was a level of attrition that could not be sustained indefinitely, particularly in the draining cat-and-mouse daylight air defence of the Reich. By this stage, the Luftwaffe found it increasingly difficult to concentrate its forces against large-scale American raids as its home defence units were scattered across the Reich, had to fly great distances to reach the bombers and required long periods to assemble into combat groupings of a size necessary to make an impact. Consequently, the Luftwaffe's piston-engined Bf 109, Fw 190, Bf 110 and Me 410 fighters were often late in intercepting the bombers, or were forced to land early as a result of fuel shortage. One fighter pilot, Willi Unger of 12.(*Sturm*)/JG 3, recalled:

> The operational bases of our fighter units in the *Reichsverteidigung* [Defence of the Reich] were spread all over Germany. Attempts to maintain strength at critical times and in critical areas were made by the rapid re-deployment of fighters to northern or southern Germany. Several *Gruppen* would combine together in the air from various airfields and were then led together from the ground to attack the

approaching bombers. This did not always work. The bombers often 'cheated' by flying towards one town, before changing their course and bombing a completely different target. As the flying endurance of our fighters with an auxiliary drop tank was maximum 2.5 hours, we were often forced to break off. There is no question of German fighters having the advantage – only disadvantages, since the numbers of American escort fighters were far superior to us and they also operated at higher altitude – to our disadvantage.

Exacerbating this situation to a fatal degree was the Allied invasion of Normandy on 6 June 1944. As a result, the bulk of the German daylight fighter force was committed to France to engage in a desperate air superiority campaign and tactical air defence, but there was still the need to provide an effective defence over the Reich – as well as the eastern and southern theatres of operations. From that point onwards, the writing was on the wall.

Nevertheless, if nothing else, the low-key arrival of the Me 262 gave a much-needed fillip to the Luftwaffe, to the *Führer*, Adolf Hitler, Reichsmarschall Hermann Göring and to the German people. When the first examples of this sleek, shark-bodied interceptor reached the Luftwaffe in the summer of 1944, they were assigned to *Erprobungskommando* (EKdo) 262, a test unit set up the previous December under the command of a former *Zerstörer* pilot, Hauptmann Werner Thierfelder, at Lechfeld, in southern Germany, specifically to assess the new aircraft.

It is important to stress that the aircraft was seen as an *interceptor* and not simply a fighter. Indeed, with a rate of climb of 1,200m per minute and a maximum speed of 845km/h at 9,000m thanks to the thrust produced by its two Junkers Jumo 004 turbines, the Me 262 was an aircraft capable of out-pacing the impressive piston-engined American P-51 Mustang. While, with drop tanks, the P-51 was able to escort the USAAF's B-17s and B-24s to Berlin and other deep-penetration targets from bases in England, its maximum speed of 438mph (705km/h) at 25,000ft (7,630m) meant that, in certain conditions, the Me 262 had the advantage.

Just over a year earlier, in April 1943, Hauptmann Wolfgang Späte, a Knight's Cross-holder and then 72-victory fighter ace, had flown the second prototype

On 17 April 1943, Me 262 V2 Wk-Nr. 262 000 0002 PC+UB, distinctive here through the absence of the aircraft's familiar nosewheel, was assessed in flight by Major Wolfgang Späte, a 72-victory recipient of the Knight's Cross. Späte subsequently reported that, in his view, with its combinaton of high performance and heavy armament, the jet fighter would be able to prove effective against both enemy fighters and bombers. However, the following day, the same machine nose-dived and crashed, killing test pilot Oberfeldwebel Wilhelm Ostertag, following an engine flame-out. (EN Archive)

An excellent view of the port side Jumo 004 jet engine of Me 262A-1a Wk-Nr. 500071 'White 3', flown by Fähnrich Hans-Guido Mütke of 9./JG 7, which force-landed in Switzerland on 25 April 1945. The Jumo 004, seen here with the aircraft rested on wooden blocks and jacks, represented the zenith of jet engine development at this time, and placed the Luftwaffe ahead of the Allies. (EN Archive)

Me 262 and reported to Generalmajor Adolf Galland, the Luftwaffe's *General der Jagdflieger* (Commanding General of the Fighter Arm), that:

> The climbing speed of the Me 262 surpasses that of the Bf 109G by 5–6m/sec. The superior horizontal and climbing speeds will enable the aircraft to operate successfully against numerically superior enemy fighters. The extremely heavy armament (six [sic] 30mm guns) permits attacks on bombers at high approach speeds with destructive results, despite the short time the aircraft is in the firing position.

Indeed, Galland recognised that the jet's superior combination of speed and armament would give the Luftwaffe the aircraft capable of evading the mass American fighter escorts in order to get through to intercept the bombers – and by June 1944, with increasing damage being inflicted on German production centres and transport hubs, this was a prime concern. He thus pushed for urgent production of the aircraft with all the leading authorities – Hitler himself, Göring, Generalfeldmarschall Erhard Milch (Secretary of the State for Aviation and Inspector General of the Luftwaffe) and Albert Speer (Minister for Armaments and War Production).

Unfortunately, EKdo 262 had barely achieved anything tangible when Thierfelder was killed on 18 July 1944 in unsubstantiated circumstances while flying a prototype Me 262 over southern Germany. Despite Hauptmann Horst Geyer assuming command the following month, in reality, this small trials unit achieved little operationally; by September it had around 12 aircraft on strength and 17 pilots – not much with which to go to war against the USAAF.

That same month Galland instigated some structural changes to the unit, assigning the staff echelon of the *Kommando* as the nucleus of a new III./EJG 2 at Lechfeld intended to oversee all future jet fighter training, while the component *Einsatzkommandos* were moved north to concrete runways at Hesepe and Achmer, which provided a suitable environment from which the jets could operate.

On paper, this appeared to be progress, but the reality was very different. Despite a strength of some 30 Me 262A-1as, most of the *Kommandos'* pilots remained largely untrained on the jet fighter, and their new bases lay directly on the approach paths of those USAAF bombers, and their escorts, which were beginning to appear in ever greater numbers in German airspace.

However, as delivery of Jumo 004 engines and production of Me 262 airframes began to gather pace, despite the Allies' best attempts to interrupt them, more jets became available. In August Galland ordered the establishment of a *Gruppe*-sized formation of three *Staffeln* each with a nominal strength of 16 Me 262s formed from the Achmer and Hesepe units with which to deploy the jet fighter on a greater scale. To lead the unit, he selected an eminent Austrian fighter ace in the form of Major Walter Nowotny, a recipient of the highest award to the Knight's Cross, the Diamonds, who was credited with 255 victories gained while flying with I./JG 54 in the East. For two of the unit's

The designer of the Me 262, Professor Willy Messerschmitt (right) with one of his senior test pilots, Fritz Wendel. Despite Messerschmitt's almost obsessive enthusiasm over the Me 262, Wendel was unimpressed by *Kommando Nowotny's* efforts to bring itself to readiness and wrote scathingly on the subject to his boss. (EN Archive)

Staffeln, pilots with experience of twin-engined aircraft and blind-flying were drawn from Me 410-equipped 8. and 9. *Zerstörergeschwader* 26, while the third was formed from scratch.

Known as *Kommando Nowotny*, the unit undertook a brief period of familiarisation and by September 1944 it had some 30 Me 262A-1s on strength. Indeed, during October, in spite of Hitler's edict to build the Me 262 as a bomber, industry had delivered a total of 52 jet *interceptors*, all but one going to Nowotny's unit. The *Kommando* went into action for the first time on 7 October against one of the largest American daylight bombing raids so far mounted, aimed at oil targets at Pölitz, Ruhland, Merseburg and Lutzkendorf. There were mixed results, with two bombers claimed shot down, although one pilot was killed and two aircraft lost as a result of being attacked by P-51s.

During the coming month, *Kommando Nowotny* fought few engagements with the USAAF as poor autumnal weather largely prevented pilots from learning how to handle the new aircraft and its advanced technology and idiosyncrasies. Ten jets were damaged during the challenging processes of taking off and landing, and only a few claims were made against the enemy. Nowotny's new pilots, most of them now drawn from conventional, single-engined fighter units, lacking sufficient training in instrument flying and with only two or three intended training flights, found the Me 262 with its effortless speed, short endurance and rapid descent difficult to master.

Despite a damning indictment on the unit's capabilities from Messerschmitt test pilot Fritz Wendel (the first man to fly the Me 262 and also part of the company's technical inspection team) and Hitler's persisting demands that the jet should fly as a high-speed bomber rather than as an interceptor, *Kommando Nowotny* struggled on into November. But on the 8th disaster struck when

Four Me 262A-1as of *Kommando Nowotny* are refuelled from a bowser on the concrete taxiway at Achmer in late 1944. The unit's pilots struggled to manage the jet interceptor's high speed and limited endurance, and after their distinguished commander, Major Walter Nowotny, was killed on 8 November, the unit was disbanded, leading to the formation of a new *Geschwader* intended to have a firm infrastructure. (EN Archive)

Nowotny crashed to his death in an Me 262, having been intercepted by American fighters on his way back from a mission.

Four days after Nowotny's death, in the wake of Hitler's eventual, semi-reluctant agreement that the jet should be built as a 'fighter' rather than as a bomber, it was decreed that a new JG 7 was to be formed, equipped not, as originally planned, with Bf 109G-14s, but rather with the Me 262A-1a and placed under the command of the former *Kommodore* of JG 77 and holder of the Knight's Cross with Oakleaves and Swords, Oberst Johannes Steinhoff. III./JG 7 was established at Lechfeld in mid-November as the initial component, with its flying and ground personnel largely being drawn from the disbanded *Kampfgeschwader* (KG) 1 '*Hindenburg*', whose honour title the new *Geschwader* would adopt for a brief period, as well as from the remains of *Kommando Nowotny*.

Steinhoff was forced to work with what he was given – and it was meagre. By the end of the month III./JG 7 had just 11 Me 262s on strength against the promised figure of 40. Eventually, in January 1945, the *Gruppe* reached its intended strength of 40 pilots, with the 9., 10. and 11. *Staffeln* transferring to their operational bases at Parchim, Oranienburg and Brandenburg-Briest, respectively. However, although pilot availability may have been acceptable, aircraft availability was still painfully lacking, with only 19 Me 262s being recorded on strength on 19 January. A planned II. *Gruppe*, to be formed from elements of III./KG 1, was redesignated on 24 November as a new IV./JG 301, with 5., 6., 7. and 8./JG 7 becoming 13., 14., 15. and 16./JG 301, respectively. This new *Jagdgruppe* was also to take over the *Hindenburg* title from JG 7.

The new *Geschwader* would fall under the tactical control of Oberst Heinrich Wittmer's 1. *Jagddivision* at Ribbeck, which, in turn, reported to I. *Jagdkorps* under Generalmajor Joachim-Friedrich Huth at Treuenbritzen, its zone of operation being northwest and central Germany.

As *Kommandeur* of III./JG 7, Steinhoff assigned 29-year-old Major Erich Hohagen. A veteran pilot who had accumulated several thousand hours flying some 60 different types, Hohagen had initially seen action on the Channel

Main Me 262 fighter bases

Neumünster
II./JG 7

Kaltenkirchen
I. and III./JG 7

Parchim
III./JG 7

NETHERLANDS

Oranienburg
I. and III./JG 7

Hesepe
Erprobungskommando 262

Achmer
Erprobungskommando 262
Kommando Nowotny

Brandenburg-Briest
Stab
I. and III./JG 7

● Berlin

GERMANY

LUXEMBOURG

CZECHOSLOVAKIA

Kitzingen
II./KG(J) 54

Giebelstadt
I./KG(J) 54

Neuburg
III./KG(J) 54

Lechfeld
Erprobungskommando 262
Kommando Nowotny
III./EJG 2
III./JG 7

München-Riem
JV 44

FRANCE

Salzburg-Maxglan
JV 44

AUSTRIA

N

0   100 miles

0   100km

Hauptmann Georg-Peter Eder became a potent Me 262 combat pilot. With experience gained flying fighters with 4./JG 51, III./JG 2, II./JG 1 and II./JG 26, he was assigned to Ekdo 262 and *Kommando Nowotny*. Eder then flew with III./JG 7, but on 22 January 1945 he was forced to bail out of his jet after being attacked by P-51 escort fighters while engaging American bombers near Bremen. He suffered severe injuries as a result. To that point Eder had 21 victories claimed while flying the Me 262, including six P-51s. He had been awarded the Oakleaves to his Knight's Cross on 25 November 1944 in recognition of his then total of 60 victories. (Author's Collection)

Front in 1940, where he was accredited with ten victories. By the time he was awarded the Knight's Cross on 5 October 1941, his tally had passed the 30 mark. In August 1943 Hohagen was appointed *Kommandeur* of I./JG 2.

Following one aerial battle over the Western Front in the autumn of 1944, Hohagen had been forced to belly-land his stricken fighter in a small field. The aircraft ploughed into a bank and Hohagen badly smashed his head on the fighter's reflector gunsight. During treatment for this injury a surgeon had to replace a piece of Hohagen's skull with plastic, allowing him to then pull the skin back together again. Even so, as Steinhoff later recalled, 'The two halves of his face no longer quite matched'.

Supposedly recovered from his injury, Hohagen was posted to command the newly-formed Me 262 training *Gruppe*, III./EJG 2, at Lechfeld in late 1944, before being assigned to lead III./JG 7. Troubled throughout this period by severe headaches as a direct result of his many wounds, he found the task of flying the new jet fighter challenging. Of Hohagen's total of 55 victories gained from more than 500 missions, 13 were four-engined bombers.

Throughout February 1945, III./JG 7 commenced its first sporadic operations against the USAAF. The *Gruppe's* account opened on the 3rd when 116 B-24s bombed the marshalling yards at Berlin-Tempelhof. Leutnant Rudolf Rademacher claimed two 'B-17s' shot down, but it is more likely these were B-24s. Oberleutnant Joachim Weber of 9./JG 7 and Oberleutnant Günther Wegmann and Karl Schnörrer of 11./JG 7 claimed one *Viermot* (a contraction of 'four-engines') each. Hauptmann Georg-Peter Eder, leading 11./JG 7, is believed to have shot down two P-47s, while Unteroffizier Anton Schöppler claimed a P-51.

But down on the ground, in the 'corridors of power', much intrigue and plotting had been taking place over the past month. Galland had fallen out of favour with Göring, the Reichsmarschall accusing him, according to Galland, of having a 'negative influence on fighter tactics, a lack of support and failure to enforce orders, for having created my own empire in the fighter arm, wrong staff policy, the removal of people I did not like and my responsibility for the bad state of the *Jagdwaffe'*. Göring effectively made Galland redundant, sent him on enforced leave, and replaced him with Oberst Gordon Gollob. Before he departed from office, however, Galland asked Göring that he be given permission 'to be employed operationally on the Me 262, not as a unit leader, but simply as a pilot. A decision was to be made during my leave'.

But Galland had his supporters. Throughout January 1945, by means of semi-covert meetings with a number of Luftwaffe generals and even senior SS officers, a small group of high-ranking fighter commanders under Oberst Günther Lützow 'mutinied' against Göring, attempting to force a meeting with him at which they intended to put forward their grievances about the unsatisfactory way the fighter arm was being run, and to demand Galland's reinstatement. This initiative proved unsuccessful, and on 23 January Göring officially announced Galland's dismissal.

The former *General der Jagdflieger* was given permission to set up his own, semi-autonomous unit of Me 262s and to take the 'mutineers' with him. By March, *Jagdverband* (JV) 44 had been established at Brandenburg-Briest essentially to 'prove' to the higher authorities that the Me 262 was an effective jet interceptor rather than a high-speed bomber, the latter role conforming to Hitler's vision of the aircraft, and to which, of course, Göring was compelled to subscribe.

In its formative phase, JV 44 numbered a handful of Luftwaffe fighter aces. These included Steinhoff, who as a leading member of the 'plot' against Göring had been relieved of his command of JG 7, and also Hohagen. They were joined by Knight's Cross-holder Major Karl-Heinz Schnell from JG 102, who was credited with more than 60 victories, Oberfeldwebel Klaus Neumann of JG 7 with 19 four-engined victories and Oberfeldwebel Franz Steiner of 2./JG 11 with 12 victories, ten of which were four-engined bombers. Finally, the unit also boasted several very experienced NCO flying instructors.

Most of March was taken up preparing JV 44, with flying being confined to a small number of Siebel Si 204s light transports in order to instruct the pilots in twin-engined take-offs and landings, instrument flying and radio familiarisation. It would not be until 14 March that JV 44 took delivery of its first Me 262s, and the unit's first combat mission is believed to have been carried out towards the end of the month. A *Kette* of three jets, led by Steinhoff and including Neumann, took off from Briest, headed over Berlin and then flew east, following the course of the road towards Frankfurt-an-der-Oder.

Approaching the Oder river and the German frontlines, the Me 262s flew into light Flak, and so descended in order to assess the situation on the ground. Turning for home a little later, the jets suddenly encountered a loose formation of Soviet fighters over the river. The *Jagdwaffe* pilots found themselves momentarily uncertain as to how best to take on the slower piston-engined aircraft in their high-speed interceptors. Steinhoff rolled his Messerschmitt over, and as he did so, he observed a formation of Il-2 *Shturmovik* ground attack aircraft strafing a German transport column a short distance away. The closing speed of his jet was too great, however, and he was only able to fire off a very short burst at one of the enemy machines from his 30mm cannon. The Me 262 was now flying very low over the forested landscape, and as he recalled, 'the tips of the tall pines almost seemed to brush the Me 262's wings'. The *Shturmovik* Steinhoff had fleetingly fired at now started to trail smoke, and it subsequently hit the ground at the edge of the treeline before bouncing along in the snow, breaking up into pieces.

Steinhoff had learned two lessons from this experience: firstly, that in handling, the Me 262 required a fine balance of speed and marksmanship, particularly in using a slow rate-of-fire heavy cannon; and secondly, that the jet consumed fuel quickly. The Me 262s returned to Briest with their tanks almost dry.

Within a short period of time JV 44 would move south to Munich-Riem, which would serve as its principal base for operations. The combat role and performance of both JG 7 and JV 44 will be explored in detail in Chapters 5 and 6.

Aside from the fighter units, from November 1944, when I./KG 51 had absorbed the Me 262 bomber test unit *Kommando Schenk*, its parent *Geschwader*, under the command of Oberstleutnant Wolfgang Schenk (and, from 1 February 1945, Oberstleutnant Rudolf Hallensleben), operated two *Gruppen* of Me 262A-2as as bombers/fighter-bombers – I./KG 51 at Volkel, Rheine and Hopsten under Major Heinz Unrau, and II./KG 51 based at Schwäbisch-Hall, Achmer and Essen-Müllheim under Hauptmann Hans-Joachim Grundmann.

Throughout the gloomy autumn of 1944, KG 51's jet bombers were engaged in intense cat-and-mouse operations against the Allied tactical air forces as, outnumbered, they struggled to provide badly needed air support to the German armies battling on the Western Front. But with their bases continually under attack from Tempest Vs of the 2nd Tactical Air Force (TAF), against which only the Me 262's speed was the saving grace, and with shortages in fuel and bombs, this was difficult.

The *Geschwader* had calculated that 65 tons of J2 fuel was needed to train just one pilot. Operations took the form of hit-and-run style missions with either 500kg bombs or AB 250 containers loaded with fragmentation bombs intended for Allied airfields. Other transport, troop and bridge targets were struck in the Liége, Antwerp, Nijmegen, Volkel and Eindhoven areas, as well as Allied troop concentrations resulting from the failed airborne assault at Arnhem. But many of KG 51's former Ju 88 and Me 410 pilots now assigned to fly the Me 262 found it a difficult and challenging task, unfamiliar as they were with the strange new jet engines, and consequently losses grew.

In addition, a small number of Me 262A-1a/U3 variants were operated as high-speed reconnaissance machines by *Kommando Braunegg*, named after its commander, Knight's Cross-holder Oberleutnant Herward Braunegg. Also known as *Kommando Panther*, the unit flew trial missions from Lechfeld and Schwäbisch Hall, their jets fitted with twin Rb 50/30 cameras in their noses in place of the standard MK 108 cannon armament. Later, this unit carried out vital reconnaissance in preparation for the *Wacht am Rhein* German counter-offensive in the Ardennes. The unit's aircraft were able to roam virtually at will over Allied lines, gathering vital photographic coverage of enemy troop dispositions and the crossings over the Meuse.

On 15 December, the *Kommando* reported a strength of 11 pilots and six Me 262A-1a/U3s. Despite this, it was rare for more than four aircraft to be operational at one time. In 1945, the small Me 262 reconnaissance force was expanded when 1. *Nahaufklärungsgruppe* (NAG) 1 and 1. and 2./NAG 6 also undertook photographic missions over the Western Front. These operations were also vital to the German high command, but again were carried out only in limited numbers.

But the real 'jet war' was yet to come when, from early 1945, JG 7 and JV 44 pitted their small number of revolutionary interceptors with their unprecedented speed and formidable firepower against the might of the Allied air forces. This would be a war of technical innovation against mass air power. It would test both sides.

CHAPTER 3
PATH TO COMBAT

Very often a marked paradox existed in the training of the Luftwaffe's Me 262 pilots. During the first five years of the war, many of the young men eventually selected to fly what was the fastest and most technically advanced aircraft in the world in 1944 would go through a formal programme which would graduate them to a level at which they were considered to be suitably trained and sufficiently competent to fly a piston-engined aircraft. And yet, ironically, by the end of 1944, when the first Me 262s were being delivered in numbers, because of growing shortages in fuel, aircraft and instructors, as well as increasingly adverse operating conditions, the Luftwaffe was almost incapable of sustaining an organised and structured training programme for the jet fighter with which it hoped to win back some degree of air superiority.

In the autumn of 1944, the 10. *Staffel* of III./EJG 2 had been formed around the remnants of EKdo 262 at Lechfeld. The intention was to establish a dedicated Me 262 operational training unit that would offer pilots converting to the jet comprehensive and thorough training. The unit was helped by the appointment of Oberstleutnant Heinz Bär, one of the *Jagdwaffe*'s most renowned fighter aces and leaders, as its commander. His service career stretched back to 1939, and subsequently after service on all major fronts he was credited with more than 190 victories and awarded the Swords and Oakleaves to the Knight's Cross. However, earlier in 1944, he had clashed with Göring and his appointment to III./EJG 2 was seen as being side-lined to some extent.

Initially, about 50 pilots were assembled from both fighter and bomber units and fighter school staffs, and a selection was made of promising new pilots who were about halfway through their operational fighter training. They were given a pre-jet flying course which consisted of finishing their regular 20 hours of flying time in conventional fighter aircraft with the throttles fixed in one position to reproduce a technical problem found in flying in the Me 262, the throttles of which were not to be adjusted in flight at high altitudes.

Upon arrival at Lechfeld, all pilots were given three days of theoretical instruction in the operation and functioning of jet engines, the features

and flying qualities of the Me 262, and some practice in operating the controls in a wingless training model. This introduction was followed by a course at Landsberg in the operation of conventional twin-engined aircraft. Pupils were given five hours of flying time in a Bf 110 and a Si 204, practising take-offs, landings, flight with the radio course indicator, instrument flying and flying on one engine. Upon completion of the course, the pilots returned to III./EJG 2 at Lechfeld, where they were given one more day of theoretical instruction prior to commencing conversion to the Me 262.

Practical instruction on the Me 262 began with a half-day exercise in starting and stopping the jet motors and taxiing. Flying instruction consisted of a total of nine take-offs to familiarise the pilot with fuel flow, aerobatics, high altitude, aerial manoeuvres, formation flying and gunnery practice. This was considered to be the minimum with which to qualify a pilot for operational readiness on the Me 262.

After a long and illustrious career on all the main battlefronts commanding several fighter units with distinction, Oberstleutnant Heinz Bär, a recipient of the Knight's Cross with Oakleaves and Swords with around 200 victories to his credit, was assigned a relatively 'backwater' position in command of the jet training *Gruppe* III./EJG 2 at Lechfeld. The bluntly-spoken ace had fallen foul of Göring, who may have eased Bär's passage away from operations. He is seen here sitting on the wing of 'Red 13', the Me 262 he tended to fly from Lechfeld. (EN Archive)

Throughout December 1944, the number of pilots undergoing training at Lechfeld increased dramatically in proportion to the number of instructors available: a total of 135 trainee pilots for only 28 instructors, although the ratio of aircraft to pilots was even lower. Training was severely restricted due to a shortage of the twin-seat training version, the Me 262B-1, and even by the end of January 1945, III./EJG 2 recorded only three such machines on strength.

Not all pilots went through III./EJG 2, however.

Eduard Schallmoser was born in the small southern German town of Aying, 20km southeast of Munich, on 4 October 1923. Like thousands of other young men of his generation in Germany during the 1930s, he had been captivated by the excitement and glamour of flight. As a boy growing up in Bavaria, he was fascinated by the stories of his uncle, Leutnant Max Riedmaier, who had flown with the *Königlich Bayerische Fliegerabteilung*, and who had been shot down over the Western Front on 30 June 1918.

Schallmoser's enthusiasm was fuelled further when, in January 1933, Adolf Hitler rose to power. The *Führer* recognised the considerable propaganda and potential military value in sports flying, and the *Nationalsozialistisches Fliegerkorps* (NSFK) – a branch of the Nazi Party – was formed in April 1937 to encourage boys from the age of 12 to learn to fly. It also incorporated the *Flieger-Hitlerjugend*, and in 1938 the 15-year-old Schallmoser eagerly joined its ranks, if for no other reason than to avoid 'military drill every Sunday!'

He embarked on a course of fieldcraft, workshop duties, physical fitness and, ultimately, glider flying.

By 1941, at the age of 18, Schallmoser had successfully attained his *Segelflugschein* (Glider Certificate) A, B and C – the three grades of glider pilot licence issued by the NSFK. He was set upon a career as a pilot, and with Germany now at war in the west and about to attack in the east, Schallmoser applied to join the Luftwaffe. In May of that year, he officially joined the service as a member of 3. *Fliegerausbildungsregiment* at Klagenfurt, with whom he embarked upon the standard course of fitness training, medical examinations, infantry training and sport.

In December 1941 Schallmoser commenced the standard radio communication and navigation course at the *Fluzeugführer-Antwärter-Bataillon* at Seyring-bei-Wien. He remarked dryly of his time there 'again, a lot of drill'. In February 1942, Schallmoser was posted to the *Flugzeugführerschule A/B 112* at Böblingen to begin his basic pilot's training, which included aerobatics (32 starts), instrument training (38 starts), formation flying (nine starts) and cross-country (44 starts). He would be fortunate enough to accumulate more than 500 hours on a variety of types including the Kl 35, Fw 44, Bü 181, He 51, Ar 96, Caudron C.445 and W 34.

A somewhat vexed-looking Major Erich Hohagen glares at the photographer from the cockpit of Me 262A-1a 'White 2' of III./EJG 2 at Lechfeld during his conversion and training period there. Lore dictated that it was considered unlucky to photograph a pilot just before a mission. (EN Archive)

Gefreiter Schallmoser's aptitude and enthusiasm was deemed sufficient enough for him to be considered as a possible instructor. In July 1943, he transferred to the *Fluglehrerschule* at Quedlinburg, where, following 84 hours spent flying C.445s, W 34s, Bü 181s and Fw 58s, he received his *Fluglehrerschein* (Flying Instructor's Certificate) and *Blindflugschein* (Blind Flying Certificate) 1. Three months later, Schallmoser returned to Böblingen as an instructor, specialising in night-flying tuition and making no fewer than 325 nocturnal instrumentation flights between November 1943 and September 1944. His period at Böblingen was briefly interrupted in May 1944 when he was posted to the *Nachtjagdschule Altenburg* for a short conversion course onto the Bf 109 as a single-seat nightfighter (with some additional hours on the Si 204 and Ar 96).

By October 1944, more qualified pilots were needed by the fighter units operating in the defence of the Reich, resulting in Unteroffizier Schallmoser's career as a flying instructor being terminated by more pressing wartime requirements. On 7 October, he was posted to the operational fighter training unit 6./JG 101 for a few days, before moving to 7./JG 112, where he was familiarised on the Bf 109F, G and the rare T variant. His *Staffelführer* wrote of his pupil, 'Intelligent and fit. Very talented. Open and knowledgeable person. Is very interested in becoming a fighter pilot'.

A stint with 12./EJG 1 at Weidengut/Breslau followed in November 1944, where Schallmoser completed 17 hours of formation flying training, air combat readiness and gunnery skills in the Bf 109G-6. Upon conclusion of his course, Schallmoser's *Staffelkapitän* was pleased with his pupil's achievements, writing:

> His take-offs and landings are faultless. He is fully conversant with the Bf 109. His combat flying capability is good. He is quiet and confident in formation flying. The result of his aerial gunnery: average. Recommended for fighter group (Me 262).

So it was that on 26 November, instead of being posted to a conventional fighter unit, Schallmoser was sent instead to 9./EJG 2 at Landsberg to begin preparatory training for the Me 262A-1a standard fighter. This involved four-and-a-half hours spent practising in the twin-engined Si 204 and Bf 110, with a further six hours in a Bü 181 for gunnery and target skills. On 10 January 1945, Schallmoser moved to Unterschlauersbach for final conversion to the Me 262 with 10./EJG 2. The training course offered at Unterschlauersbach at this time comprised:

Circuits – three starts/1.5 hours
Altitude flights (12,000m) – two starts/two hours
Navigation training – one start/45 minutes
Formation flying – one start/30 minutes

Obergefreiter Eduard Schallmoser, as photographed in his paybook while undergoing training at the *Fluglehrerschule* Quedlinburg in the summer of 1943. He would later be assigned to training on the Me 262, and would see combat with JV 44. (Author's Collection, courtesy of Schallmoser)

As with his earlier training, Schallmoser impressed his instructor at Lechfeld with his flying abilities:

> A big, tall man with quiet mannerisms; open and honest in character. Considerable operational awareness. In his circle of comrades, he is well liked. Promises to make a good fighter pilot. Possesses strong emotions about flying. Converted onto Si 204 and Bf 110 with no problems whatsoever. Take-offs and landings very consistent. Flies single engine like a model. Precision landing is good. Strongly recommended for the Me 262.

With the successful completion of his training, Eduard Schallmoser received his posting to JV 44 on 2 March 1945, and the next day he travelled to Brandenburg-Briest, where the unit was in the process of forming up. A month later, JV 44 transferred south to Munich-Riem with orders to defend the jet aircraft production facilities in southern Germany, Schallmoser accompanying Generalleutnant Galland in a Si 204.

The 'training programme' at Munich-Riem was dictated by the paucity of Me 262s, the interruption and danger caused by Allied bombing attacks and erratic fuel availability. Nevertheless, Galland and Steinhoff persevered as best they could with some kind of rudimentary instruction. One of the most notable names to join Galland's unit at this time was Hauptmann Walter Krupinski, who had flown more than 1,100 operational missions during which

he had been accredited with 197 confirmed victories, having been five times wounded, bailed out on four occasions and survived numerous crash-landings. By March 1945, Krupinski, a recipient of the Knight's Cross with Oakleaves, had effectively been made redundant by the continual regroupings and redesignations of the various Luftwaffe fighter *Geschwader*.

Krupinski's 'training' on the Me 262 began in earnest on 2 April 1945 at Riem. A lone Me 262 was hauled out onto the concrete start platform on the western edge of the airfield. Steinhoff was the 'instructor'. Krupinski remembers:

That morning, I sat in the cockpit of an Me 262 at Riem. I had a hell of a bad head, the result of too many drinks the night before! Steinhoff was standing on the port wing. He said, 'The most difficult thing with this type of aircraft is to start the engines. I'll do that for you'. There was no reading any books or anything like that. There was no 'training programme'. He just gave me some basic information, enough to get started. 'It's very tricky', he said. 'On take-off, you need a very long time until you get airborne. Don't do anything in a hurry. On landing, it's the other way around: you can't get the speed back down to a normal landing speed. She's fast, very fast!'

Actually, I found that taking off in the Me 262 was fairly easy because the nose wheel rolled nice and smoothly, but the problem, as Steinhoff had said, was that the engines didn't accelerate and bring up speed fast enough. You needed the whole length of the airfield before you reached an adequate take-off speed. At Riem, the strip we used was about 1,100m long, and only after about 1,000m did you have the lifting speed to come off the field.

Anyway, I prepared myself for take-off; I closed the canopy, threw a quick glance over the instrument panel. Brakes off. Slowly, like a lame duck, the bird began to

Oberfeldwebel Hermann Buchner crouches on the join between the wing leading edge and port jet engine of Me 262A-1a 'White 7' and speaks to one of the groundcrew during his training at Lechfeld on 20 October 1944. Buchner, a successful former Fw 190 ground-attack pilot, made the relatively rare transition to flying the Me 262 and was credited with 12 victories on the type, ranking him as the seventh highest-scoring German jet pilot. He was awarded the Knight's Cross in July 1944 for 46 aerial victories – an exceptional tally for a ground-attack pilot. (EN Archive)

Hauptmann Walter Krupinksi, photographed wearing the Knight's Cross with Oakleaves which he was awarded on 2 March 1944, having been accredited with 174 victories. By March 1945, he found himself being rested after exhaustion, having flown more than 1,000 missions. Krupinski's subsequent 'transition' to the Me 262 was both unexpected and rudimentary. (Author's Collection, courtesy of Krupinski)

roll. But then the end of the runway, as I predicted, came towards me very quickly. A glance at the speed indicator told me I was moving at 200km/h. Pulling gently at the stick, I got into the air. No drag, and she climbed swiftly. Landing-gear up. Throttle lightly back to 8,000rpm. I climbed and the speed grew and grew: 350, 400, 500, 600km/h – there seemed no end to its speed. Still I climbed. It was fantastic! Nothing like the Bf 109. For my first roll in the climb I used only ailerons, moving with lightning speed; neither rudder nor thrust were needed, and at 6,000 or 7,000m I levelled out, the speed slowly approaching 900km/h. So there I was, flying on my first mission, though I suppose it was more of a solo transition flight really.

Comparatively, the training situation at JG 7 was marginally better. When Messerschmitt test pilot Fritz Wendel visited the *Geschwader* at Brandenburg-Briest in early 1945 as part of the company's technical inspection team (by which time Steinhoff's successor, Major Theo Weissenberger, was in command), he was impressed by the fact that what he termed as 'safe flying' training was being undertaken. Indeed, Wendel saw pilots using radio aids for navigational purposes and, astonishingly, formation flying in *Gruppe* strength. However, by the end of February, at Parchim at least, things had changed, as Leutnant Walter Hagenah of 9./JG 7 described:

By the time I reached JG 7, there were insufficient spare parts and insufficient engines and there were occasional shortages of fuel. I am sure all of these things were available somewhere, but by that stage of the war the transport system was so chaotic that things often failed to arrive at the frontline units. We were not even allowed to look inside the cowling of the jet engines because we were told that they were secret and we did not "need to know" what was there!

The real danger in being sent straight to an operational unit, however, was that one could do no training if there were not enough serviceable aircraft for operations. Our 'ground school' lasted for about one afternoon. We were told about the peculiarities of the jet engine, the danger of a flame-out at high altitude and the poor acceleration at low altitude. Then we were told of the vital importance of handling the throttles carefully, or else the engine might catch fire.

On the day before my first flight in the Me 262, I had a brief flight in a Si 204 to practice twin-engine handling and asymmetric flying. Next morning, 25 March 1945, I made my first familiarisation flight in the rear seat of a two-seat Me 262B – precisely 17 minutes, and accompanied by a weapons technician/instructor from Brandenburg-Briest. I was greatly impressed by the Me 262.

The take-off was easy, the visibility from the cockpit was marvellous after the tail-down Bf 109 and Fw 190, and there was no propeller torque. The only real problem I found was that when I came into land, I approached at normal speed, expecting the speed to fall away rapidly when the throttle was closed. But the

A groundcrewman leans over to fasten the canopy of an Me 262A-1a of III./JG 7 at Brandenburg-Briest. The canopy hinged open on the starboard side of the aircraft. This machine is Wk-Nr. 111892. Note the last three digits of the Werknummer visible on the tail assembly and the blue and red defence of the Reich unit identification band on the rear fuselage, onto which has been marked the vertical bar of III. *Gruppe.* (EN Archive)

Me 262 was such a clean machine. We had been warned before take-off not to throttle back to less than 6,000rpm; we were also told, when turning on the base leg for landing, not to do so at less than 300km/h. The important thing was to make up your mind in good time whether you were going to land or throw away that approach and try another. If you throttled back and the engine revolutions fell too low, they would not accelerate quickly enough if you tried to open up and go round again. Brandenburg-Briest had a concrete runway, and jets could set fire to tarmac!

Once you began to exceed 900 km/h, the Me 262 did not 'feel right' – you did not have complete control of it as it drifted from side to side, and there was the feeling you would lose control if you took it much faster.

Generally, training was unbelievably short – just an afternoon's chat and a short morning's accompanied flight, then, in the afternoon, one went solo. We had some pilots with only about 100 hours total flying time on our unit flying the Me 262. Whilst they might have been able to take-off and land the aircraft, I had the definite impression that they would have been little use in combat.

Just how effective or successful these hasty attempts at training the Luftwaffe's pilots on the jet interceptor were would be proved in the skies over Germany in the last three months of the war.

CHAPTER 4
WEAPON OF WAR

Since the late 1930s German aircraft designers and engineers had been at work developing an innovative new aerial propulsion technology in the form of the turbojet engine. It had been the Heinkel company which had first got an aircraft powered by jet engines into the air when the He 178 V1 flew for the first time on 27 August 1939 fitted with a 500kp-thrust HeS 3b engine. In February of the following year, Ernst Heinkel's contemporary, Professor Willy Messerschmitt, had enhanced the design of his P.1065, a project which had been intended to fulfil a specification issued by the *Reichsluftfahrtministerium* (RLM) dating from January 1939 calling for a high-speed interceptor capable of a maximum speed of 900km/h and to be powered by a single, unspecified jet engine.

Initially, the P.1065 featured a wing virtually identical in planform to the Bf 109 fighter, but in February 1940 it was modified to have its outer wing sections swept back some 18 degrees in order to solve problems that heavier engine weight estimates caused on the positioning of the aircraft's centre of gravity. Furthermore, it was believed, correctly, that swept wings would reduce the component of airspeed perpendicular to the leading edge, avoiding sharp rises in turbulence and drag.

In order to get the prototype P.1065 flying as soon as possible, it was proposed to fit the aircraft with a single 700hp Junkers Jumo 210G piston engine in the nose, using a similar installation to that of the Bf 109D. Then, as soon as they became available, two BMW P.3302 turbojet engines were to be mounted under the wings.

After wind tunnel-testing had shown that sweeping the wing back improved the aircraft's limiting Mach number, a proposal was issued on 4 April 1941 to develop a 35-degree swept-back wing with an area of 20 square metres and a span of ten metres. Construction of the first P.1065 prototype took place between February and March 1941, the project receiving the official RLM designation 'Me 262' on 8 April.

Messerschmitt's state-of-the-art fighter took to the air using pure jet power on 18 July 1942 when company test pilot Fritz Wendel made a trouble-free flight

Messerschmitt test pilot Fritz Wendel climbs out of the cockpit of the Me 262 V3 prototype PC+UC following an engine test run at Leipheim in 1943, the aircraft having been rebuilt following an accident during trials the previous year. The V3 reached unprecedented test speeds in the autumn of 1943. (EN Archive)

from Leipheim in the V3. The prototype was fitted with a pair of Jumo 004A-0 (T1) engines. Despite the delayed gestation of both aircraft and powerplant, Wendel was able to report generally smooth handling of the Me 262 during the maiden test-flight, and he achieved an unprecedented airspeed of 720km/h. Regardless of any misgivings he may have harboured, Wendel also recorded that the Junkers T1 engines 'worked well'.

From then until mid-1944, development on the Me 262 forged ahead using a series of prototypes to test all aspects of the aircraft. Low points were encountered when some of the early prototypes crashed and two test pilots were killed. Despite these setbacks, Generalmajor Galland was greatly enthused when he flew the V4 in May 1943 at Lechfeld and made his famous report to Göring in which he proclaimed, 'It felt as if angels were pushing!' As far as performance was concerned, even in its prototype variants, the Me 262 was, indeed, a formidable and ground-breaking aircraft. As early as October 1943, the V3 was achieving test speeds of 950km/h, whilst eight months later, the Me 262 S2 reached 1,004km/h in a dive. In terms of offensive load, it was planned to install one 30mm MK 103 cannon and two 20mm MG 151/20 cannon in the nose of the aircraft.

Galland became a firm advocate for the further development of the jet, and he wrote to his superiors that all measures should be taken to ensure swift mass production of the aircraft. In a report to the *Generalluftzeugmeister*, Generalfeldmarschall Erhard Milch, he wrote:

> The aircraft represents a great step forward and could be our greatest chance; it could guarantee us an unimaginable lead over the enemy if he adheres to the piston engine. The flying qualities of the airframe make a very good impression. The engines are extremely convincing, except during take-off and landing. The aircraft opens completely new tactical possibilities.

Galland's enthusiasm may have been a little premature, for at around the same time, the director of testing at Messerschmitt, Dipl.-Ing. Gerhard Caroli, offered his own appraisal of the Me 262 in which he warned, amongst other

As commanding general of the Luftwaffe fighter arm, Adolf Galland, seen here as a Major and wearing the Knight's Cross with Oakleaves and Swords, was an ardent champion of the Me 262 from the first time he flew it in May 1943. He believed that the jet interceptor would provide the Luftwaffe with the aircraft it needed to take on the Allied strategic air forces over Europe from early 1944, especially in terms of being able to evade the Spitfire and Mustang escorts and then shoot down four-engined bombers with the minimum expenditure of ammunition. (Author's Collection, courtesy of Galland)

things, of problematical ailerons, high forces on the elevators and rudders, inadequate directional stability, poor stall behaviour and insufficient fuel injection. But Galland won Milch's support, and immediate priority was given to an initial Me 262 building programme. It encountered problems from the start. An American air raid on the Regensburg assembly plant in August destroyed crucial fuselage jigs and acceptance gauges and forced the company to relocate its project office from Augsburg to Oberammergau, in the Bavarian Alps. Also, the promised 1,800 skilled workers needed to tool-up production lines arrived late, resulting in the loss of almost three million man hours in nine months.

On 2 November 1943, Göring and Milch visited the bomb-damaged Regensburg works and met Messerschmitt. It was at this meeting that a new, previously unforeseen dimension crept in – Adolf Hitler. Göring demanded of Messerschmitt whether the Me 262 could carry bombs externally. '*Herr* Reichsmarschall', Messerschmitt replied, 'It was intended from the beginning that the machine could be fitted with two bomb racks so that it could drop bombs, either one 500kg or two 250kg. But it can also carry one 1,000kg or two 500kg bombs'. Göring was elated. 'That answers the *Führer*'s question'.

Three days later, Göring and Milch were at Dessau, where they met Dr. Anselm Franz of the Junkers engine company. Bombs or no bombs, an aircraft cannot fly without engines. The design of the Me 262 incorporated a pair of Jumo 004 turbojet engines mounted beneath the wings, each unit comprising an eight-stage axial flow compressor, six separate combustion chambers and a single-stage turbine. The first production engines were delivered in May 1943, having been improved by modifications to the compressor and the turbine entry nozzles which increased static thrust from 840kg to 900kg. Two months later, however, it was noticed that there were still 'inconsistencies' in engine performance, with the engines on the V3 and V4 prototypes suffering from burning after shutdown.

The summer was dogged by flame-outs and leaking and igniting fuel, and Franz informed Göring and Milch during their visit to Dessau of difficulties still being experienced with individual components, including the turbine wheel which suffered from vibration, and the control system, where there was difficulty in opening and closing the throttles. 'It cannot be guaranteed with certainty', Franz admitted, 'That we will have the problem at upper altitudes rectified by the time series production begins so that the pilot will be able to open and close the throttles without worrying about a flame-out'.

Göring seems to have been unworried by this, for on 26 November he invited Hitler to Insterburg, in East Prussia, so that he could view a display of some of the Luftwaffe's latest aircraft and weaponry. At one point the Me 262 V6 streaked past flown by Flugkapitän Gerd Lindner. Hitler was impressed. He enquired whether the aircraft was able to carry bombs. Messerschmitt, also in attendance, eagerly stepped forward and again reiterated that the jet could carry a bomb-load of 1,000kg. Shortly afterwards, Göring duly ordered the necessary trials to commence.

That Hitler asked if the Me 262 was able to carry bombs may have been a misguided question from a man who had little appreciation of air strategy and aircraft design, but, at the same time, it was understandable, since every other Luftwaffe combat aircraft had proved itself capable of carrying bombs or performing in the fighter-bomber role. What was different about the Me 262? Yet, six months later, in May 1944, on the Obersalzberg, Hitler had discovered from Milch that contrary to his orders that the Me 262 be produced exclusively as a fighter-bomber, the aircraft was, in fact, being built purely as a fighter/interceptor. Hitler was exasperated and flew into a rage. Milch tried to reason, '*Führer*, even the smallest child can see that this is a fighter and not a bomber'.

However, Galland managed to maintain some influence over the development programme, steering the Me 262 towards deployment as a fighter/interceptor. The Me 262 eventually emerged as a twin-engined jet interceptor powered by two Jumo 004 turbojet units. Indeed, the main variant to see operational service was the A-1a daylight interceptor.

The first attempt at defining standardisation came on 8 May 1943 when Messerschmitt engineers at Augsburg set out the planned production models: the A-1 fighter and the A-2 fighter-bomber. At this time, the Me 262 was still deep in its prototype testing phase, although it had been agreed that the 'A' variant was to be an all-metal, single-seater with swept-back wings, powered by two turbojet units.

Fearful of the appearance of Allied jet aircraft, Professor Messerschmitt wrote to the production director of the Jumo engine plant at Dessau on 25 April 1944 imploring him to overcome problems and delays associated with delivery of the badly needed Jumo 004 engines: 'It is a matter of life and death for us all to set up the numbers of Me 262s with your engines as rapidly as possible'. It was therefore remarkable, in view of Allied bombing of the transport network, production centres and airfields, and the ensuing production bottlenecks, that the Me 262A-1a, a fighter formed of entirely new concepts in aeronautical design and technology, reached the Luftwaffe within three months of Messerschmitt's letter.

In its standard form the Me 262A-1a was an elegant, low-wing, all-metal, twin-jet, single-seat interceptor with 18.5-degree swept-back wings bearing a span of 12.56m, a shark-like fuselage 10.6m in length incorporating a nosewheel, and a large, high, tail assembly to which were fitted horizontal stabilisers also with swept-back

The shark-like fuselage, jet engine intakes, nosewheel, cannon barrel ports and high horizontal stabilisers are seen to advantage in this photograph of Me 262A-1a 'White 5' Wk-Nr. 111745 of JV 44, seen parked at the unit's 'start area' at Munich-Riem in the spring of 1945. (Author's Collection)

Major Erich Hohagen sits at the controls of an Me 262A-1a in a still from an instructional film using aircraft and pilots of III./EJG 2 at Lechfeld. The pilot was accommodated in a self-contained sub-assembly which held the instrument panel, electrical controls, stick and rudder, throttles, seat and battery. This *Wanne* (tub) was designed to break free on impact in the case of a crash-landing, offering the pilot some degree of enclosed protection. (EN Archive)

leading edges. The equipped weight, allowing for a pilot, ammunition and a fuel load of just over 1,800 litres, was 6,074kg.

The pilot was accommodated in a self-contained sub-assembly which held the instrument panel and electrical controls, stick and rudder, throttles, seat and battery. This *Wanne* (tub) was designed to break free on impact in the case of a crash-landing, offering the pilot some degree of enclosed protection. The cockpit was capped by a hinged, all-round-vision, canopy.

The instrument panel held a large number of gauges and dials, but was well laid-out. The key flying gauges such as the airspeed indicator, altimeter, compass, turn-and-bank indicator, artificial horizon and rate of climb indicator were located on a panel to the left, while engine controls, injection and gas pressure, and temperature indicators were grouped to the right. An arm-level panel to the left of the pilot housed the undercarriage and oxygen controls, with radio and electrics on a similar panel to the right. Ahead of an operational flight the pilot would check whether his seat was locked to a sufficient height, for when banking at high speeds he could be pressed down into the seat and be unable to see forward over the Revi 16B reflector gunsight.

In the standard interceptor configuration, the Me 262 was armed with four 30mm MK 108 cannon mounted in the nose with a total of 360 rounds (for further information, see Chapter 5). The A-1a was provided with a FuG 16ZY VHF transceiver and a FuG 25a *Erstling* IFF set suitable for day fighter operations.

The two Junkers Jumo 004B-1 turbojet engines were each comprised of an eight-stage axial compressor with single-stage turbines producing 8.8kN of thrust at 8,700rpm. The B-series engine saw improvements over the A-series, which had powered the early Me 262 prototypes. The Jumo 004B-1 included modified compressor construction using a rotor with separate discs, the replacement of castings with sheet metal where possible, improved entry to the air intake and the substitution of more than half the weight of strategic material used in the A-series engine (although solid turbine blades were still fitted). A Jumo 004 unit was 3.8m long and weighed between 730–750kg. These ground-breaking, state-of-the-art engines gave the Me 262 a climbing speed of 10m/sec at 6,000m (seven minutes) and 5.2m/sec at 9,000m (14 minutes). Maximum range when at 6,000m was 520km and in excess of 644km at 9,000m.

Standard fuel tankage totalled 2,570 litres of J2 fuel contained in four internal tanks, with provision for two ETC 503 external racks each holding a 300-litre drop tank. J2 was a brown, low-grade coal oil fuel similar to diesel oil, and it was usually available in ready supply in 1944 despite transport problems.

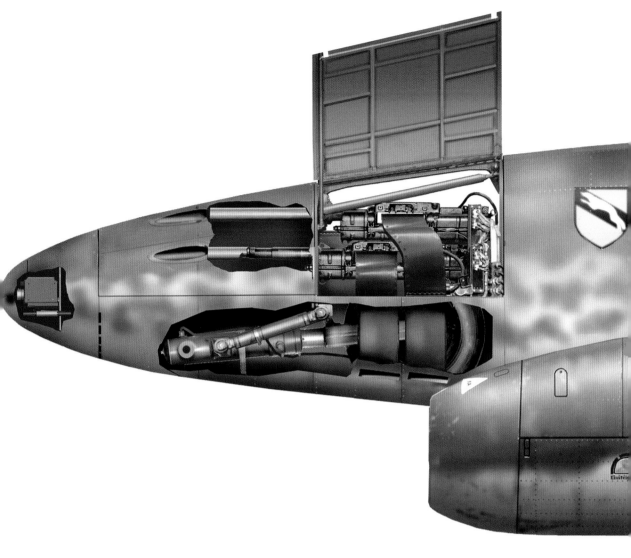

Me 262A-1a CANNON ARMAMENT

Four Rheinmetall-Borsig MK 108 30mm cannon were installed into the nose of the Me 262A-1a just above the nosewheel housing. An electric ignition cable can be seen at the rear of the installation, as can the ammunition discharge chutes. A total of 60 rounds was fed by means of a disintegrating belt from an ammunition canister mounted above the gun. Two basic types of shells could be loaded into the MK 108 – high-explosive 'Mine' shells and high-explosive incendiary shells. The MK 108 quickly earned a fearsome reputation amongst both German pilots and Allied bomber crews, the latter dubbing it the 'pneumatic hammer', but while effective when used well, the belt-fed weapon had a slow rate of fire and was prone to jamming.

Before its Jumo 004 turbines were started up, the aircraft had to be moved so that it faced the wind. Then the outboard battery was connected. Once in the cockpit, the pilot would then press the automatic switches for the left and right dynamos and starter and jet unit ignitions, as well as activating the gunsight and main instrument panel. He would check undercarriage controls, trimming, oxygen and compressed air pressures, that the fuel safety cock was

Jet effluent streams from the starboard Jumo 004 of an Me 262 of EKdo 262 as it is started up at Lechfeld in the summer of 1944. Despite their advanced technology, the jet engines could prove troublesome to the ill-trained, being prone to flame-outs, fires and stalling, while sub-standard finishing often resulted in failed components. (EN Archive)

in the 'off' position and the throttle at 'stop' and, finally, that there were no obstructions in front of or behind the aircraft.

If all was clear, to start the jet unit he would press the starter button for three to five seconds, then pull the switch, allowing the Riedel starter motor to reach 800rpm. He then pressed a black button on the throttle to activate the ignition, with the throttle held on 'stop'. At 2,000rpm he turned off the Riedel motor and opened the fuel safety cock, then switched on the fuel tank pump. The throttle was then slowly advanced to the idling position at 3,000rpm, keeping an eye on the temperature; if it exceeded 700°C he would throttle back immediately. The ignition button was then released, the outboard battery switched off and the emergency switch activated.

The Me 262 was then taxied with the Jumo turbines turning at a constant speed between 4,000–6,000rpm and with the aid of the brakes. If the aircraft was taxied too slowly, steering the nosewheel became difficult. If a turn had to be made with the assistance of the jet engines, the throttle was advanced slowly, avoiding any violent application, before entering the turn.

Immediately prior to take-off, the FuG 16ZY and FuG 25A were checked. Trimming was set at 0 degrees, or at +2 to +3 degrees with full auxiliary tanks.

For take-off, revolutions were increased to 8,000rpm, the brakes released and full throttle applied. The nosewheel was raised slightly at 160km/h and the aircraft left the ground at between 180–200km/h. Once the Me 262 was airborne, the pilot braked until the wheels were stationary and then retracted the undercarriage. When the indicator lamp signalled 'retracted', he retracted the landing flaps. Climbing to 4,000m was undertaken at 450km/h; from 4,000–6,000m at 500km/h; from 6,000–8,000m at 550km/h; and from 8,000–10,000m at between 600–650km/h.

The Me 262 was most vulnerable to Allied fighter attack when it came in to land. For this procedure the pilot had to reduce speed to 350km/h and lower the undercarriage (which produced a loud rush of air through drag), before turning in to land. He also had to press the nose down slightly to avoid the aircraft rearing up. He then lowered landing flaps to 20° and trimmed the aircraft. As the pilot turned into the field, he reduced speed to 250km/h to glide in with about 6,000–7,000rpm so that the jet units could be re-opened if necessary. Depending on height, landing flaps were lowered completely. Speed was reduced to 220km/h. A normal three-point landing followed, and once on the ground, the aircraft would tilt over onto its nosewheel.

The bomber version of the Me 262 emerged as the A-2, which, in its standard form,

The Revi (*Reflexvisier*) 16B gunsight was a standard fitting in the Me 262A-1a. Here, it is seen lowered and locked away to the right of the instrument panel. The gunsight was raised for its combat setting and the reflector glass panel pulled up. The sight incorporated a sun visor, night vision filter, light bulb and dimmer switch. Just below the sight in this photograph at the top of the instrument panel are seen, from left to right, the variometer and the tachometers. (EN Archive)

was to be equipped with two ETC 503 A-1 bomb racks beneath the forward fuselage and a Revi 16D reflector sight primarily designed for use with the reduced armament of two nose-mounted MK 108s. For bombing missions, the aircraft was to carry one 500kg or two 250kg bombs, or the equivalent weight in containers loaded with two-kilogramme anti-personnel fragmentation bombs. There was no downward-looking bombsight, but after training it was felt that pilots would become accustomed to using the Revi for bombing.

According to RLM technicians in Berlin in early June 1944, the Me 262A-2a required a landing area of 1,500m x 400m, permanent taxi tracks of 12m in width, minimum obstacle clearance of 1:70 (and, if possible, 1:100) and a 'supplementary fuel installation' of 300 cubic metres, of which 100 cubic metres should be stored near to the take-off point.

The reconnaissance role would be performed by an interim variant – a *Behelfsaufklärer*, the Me 262A-1a/U3 – a modification of the standard interceptor. This design would feature two Rb 50/30 cameras in the nose, angled outwards at 11 degrees, controlled by an intervalometer with an attached drive motor. Because the cameras were too large to fit cleanly within the nose compartment, horizontal teardrop fairings were fitted to both left and right gun access panels to cover the protruding areas and the usual gun ports found on the A-1a were faired over. Two small square glazed panels were provided for the camera lenses beneath the fuselage on either side of the nosewheel well. The variant also incorporated a FuG 16 ZS radio transceiver that operated on German army frequencies, and the aircraft had a single MK 108 cannon mounted in the extreme nose, with its muzzle protruding level with the tip.

Because of its superior speed in comparison to Allied fighters, the Me 262 was an ideal aircraft to provide short-range reconnaissance.

CHAPTER 5
ART OF WAR

By late 1944, in many respects the lives and practices of the Luftwaffe's Me 262 interceptor *Jagdflieger* resembled those of the pilots of RAF Fighter Command defending southern England from German attack four years earlier during the summer of 1940. They were indeed a 'few', trained hurriedly before being assigned to a small number of *Staffeln* comprised of limited numbers. They would spend much of their time waiting in primitive conditions for an *Alarmstart* ('scramble') order to intercept formations of enemy bombers sent to bomb their cities, airfields and factories, and these would invariably be accompanied by squadrons of escort fighters. The jet pilots were always outnumbered and out-gunned, but at least they were operating over home territory, even if their combat endurance was limited as a result of their aircraft's thirsty Jumo engines.

As mentioned previously, in terms of interceptors, from early 1945, the Luftwaffe was able to call upon a single *Jagdgeschwader* of Me 262s – JG 7 – which it based on airfields clustered across northern Germany. From there the unit could deploy its jets against Allied bombers striking at the Baltic ports, at key factories, at aircraft and synthetic oil plants in central Germany, and at Berlin. From early April, Generalleutnant Adolf Galland's composite unit of outcast aces and instructors, JV 44, became operational in Munich, but the unit could only ever draw on a small number of serviceable Me 262s and a handful of pilots.

Also in southern Germany, at Lechfeld, was Major Heinz Bär's III./EJG 2, but the primary function of this *Gruppe* was operational training, and so, wherever possible, encounters and engagements with the enemy were minimised.

The memoirs of Johannes Steinhoff portray the initial weeks of establishment of JG 7 at Brandenburg-Briest, to the west of Berlin, as being almost surreal. On one hand, the area had been left ruined by Allied bombing and a great proportion of the population had been forced to evacuate, leaving gardens to grow wild, while according to the former *Kommodore*, the 'shabby trams offered little temptation to hit town with our ration books'. Yet Steinhoff also recalled

that the unit had access to an abundance of food, as well as 'plenty of brandy, champagne and red wine, and plenty of cigarettes and cigars'.

The pilots of JG 7 were quartered either in Luftwaffe accommodation buildings at their airfield, usually simple, single-storey, wooden structures, or were billeted amongst the local population and then bussed to their bases each morning. Once at the airfield, they would eat a light, communal breakfast and then wait in chairs until *Sitzbereitschaft* (cockpit readiness) was ordered by the *Gruppe* staff. When word came through from 1. *Jagddivision* that the bombers had entered their sector, the pilots would check their aircraft and then wait at cockpit readiness until ordered to take off.

JG 7 fell under the tactical control of Oberst Heinrich Wittmer's 1. *Jagddivision* at Ribbeck, some 45km to the north of Briest, which, in turn, reported to I. *Jagdkorps* under Generalmajor Joachim-Friedrich Huth, headquartered at Treuenbritzen, lying between Berlin and Leipzig.

In the south, as commander of JV 44, Galland set up his personal quarters in a local forester's lodge and his pilots accommodated themselves in villages around the airport at Riem, on the western edge of Munich. A battle headquarters, or *Gefechtsstand*, was established in a former orphanage at Feldkirchen, three kilometres from the airport, which also had enough space to house an operations room, stores, accommodation and vehicle shelter.

The orphanage also boasted a large dining area in which pilots would partake in communal meals whilst sat at a very long table – the room also had great doors that opened out onto lawns. Pilots would hang their belts and pistols over coat hooks fitted to the wall, before taking their seat to dine. Breakfasts were a casual affair, but evening meals were arranged according to a formal seating plan, with Galland and his staff sitting on one side of the table – with Galland at the centre – while the pilots sat opposite. Food and drink was served by specially assigned orderlies.

Me 262 'Red S', believed to be from JV 44 at Brandenburg-Briest in March 1945, is readied for flight. (EN Archive)

Photographed at Munich-Riem in the spring of 1945, Oberst Johannes Steinhoff, the former *Kommodore* of JG 7 but, by this stage, effectively the operations officer of JV 44, casts a glance at some activity on the airfield. To the right, wearing sunglasses, is Leutnant Gottfried Fährmann, Steinhoff's erstwhile adjutant and wingman from JG 77, who also subsequently joined JV 44. (Author's Collection)

The danger and effect of Allied air power can be seen in this photograph – note the large bomb crater in the foreground, behind which is Me 262A-1a Wk-Nr. 110588, 'White 5' of 11./JG 7 at Brandenburg-Briest in March 1945. (EN Archive)

JV 44's Me 262s lined up at their dispersal at Munich-Riem in the spring of 1945. The unit's unique mix of aces, unit commanders and instructors flew their jets with some success against USAAF tactical bomber units of the Twelfth and Fifteenth Air Forces, although usually only in limited numbers. (Author's Collection)

Hauptmann Werner Gutowski, a veteran of the Channel battles of 1940 who had later flown with the *Geschwaderstab* of JG 77 in Italy under Steinhoff before being assigned to the *Stab General der Jagdflieger*, was subsequently assigned as JV 44's adjutant. He set up the operations room at Feldkirchen. Soon, one of the great, high-ceilinged rooms of the orphanage was fitted with a large glass panel, beneath which was a detailed map of southern Germany and Austria on which Gutowski would plot the unit's operations and enemy incursions. The surface of the glass was divided into a grid of squares stretching from Munich to Augsburg, Regensburg and Nuremberg, with each city labelled in red crayon.

On the airfield at Riem, JV 44's dispersal area comprised a primitive wooden hut close to where the Me 262s were lined up against a long, curving blast wall. Steinhoff recalled:

> The squadron's mess area was a masterpiece of improvisation, consisting basically of a table and a few rickety chairs set up in the middle of a patch of weeds and undergrowth. A field telephone stood on the table. The pilots lounged in deckchairs sipping coffee out of chunky Wehrmacht cups. Saucers of thin red jam and a stack of damp army bread covered some of the cup rings on the stained table top and provided our sustenance.'

A motorcycle was used for the transport of messages around the field.

It must be stressed that the prime role of the Me 262 was to get to the bombers using their speed and weight of armament, which included not only the MK 108 cannon, but also batteries of wing-mounted 55mm R4M rockets that were to be used specifically against the bombers, although the rockets were not always in plentiful supply. However, this in itself meant that getting

into an effective attack position at a range of about 1,000m on a dead-level approach was often challenging.

Manufactured by Rheinmetall-Borsig, the MK 108 was a blow-back operated, rear-seared, belt-fed cannon, using electric ignition, being charged and triggered by compressed air. The prime benefit of this weapon, used profusely by the Luftwaffe for close-range anti-bomber work from early 1942 onwards, lay in its simplicity and economic process of manufacture, the greater part of its components consisting of pressed sheet metal stampings.

With the advent of massed American daylight bomber formations bristling with concentrated defensive firepower, the need arose for a long-range, heavy calibre gun with which a German pilot could target specific bombers, expend the least amount of ammunition, score a kill in the shortest possible time and yet stay beyond the range of the defensive guns. It was a virtually impossible requirement, and yet the MK 108

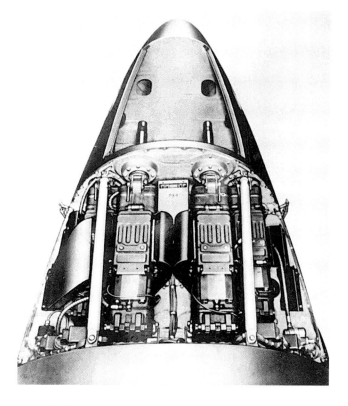

Standard installation of four 30mm MK 108 cannon in the nose of an Me 262A-1a. The lower pair of guns were set slightly forward and outboard of the upper pair. (EN Archive)

almost achieved this when used by later variants of the Bf 109 and the Fw 190A-8. It quickly earned a fearsome reputation amongst Allied bomber crews. Two types of shells could be loaded – the 30mm high-explosive tracer type 'M' shell designed to cause blast effect, and the 30mm high-explosive incendiary shell.

Generalleutnant Adolf Galland recalled the gun being installed in the Me 262s of JV 44:

Firstly, in terms of construction, it was extraordinarily easy to install four MK 108s into the aircraft. Secondly, it was good to have a gun which solved all our problems; that is to say a gun which had a rapid rate of fire and great destructive effect, although there was the disadvantage of an insufficiently flat trajectory. There were snags – the guns were not that much good when you were banking because the

The Me 262A-1a carried four air-cooled, belt-fed, 30mm MK 108 cannon in its nose. Seen here positioned upright next to the cannon are an incendiary shell (at left) and a *Minengeschoss* (mine shell) marked with an 'M'. Such ammunition was used, respectively, to cause fire in fuel tanks and blast effect within a bomber's fuselage. In the 'M' shell the upper part of the round contained the fuse, detonator, booster, explosive and closing plug. Also seen is the wire to which was attached the firing solenoid. (Author's Collection)

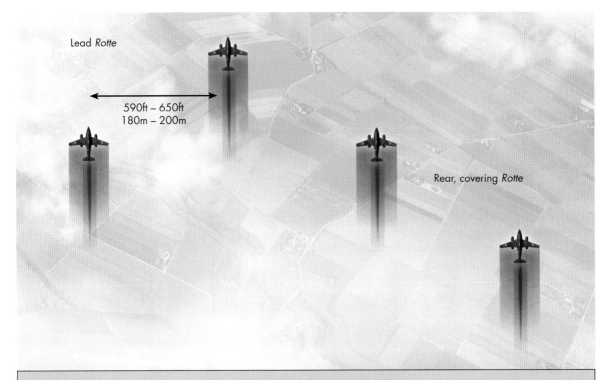

Lead *Rotte*

590ft – 650ft
180m – 200m

Rear, covering *Rotte*

Me 262 *SCHWARM* FORMATION

The standard four-aircraft *Schwarm* fighter formation evolved from the earlier three-aircraft *Kette* as used by pilots of the *Legion Condor* during the Spanish Civil War and later favoured by the Me 262 for tactical flexibility. The *Schwarm*, as employed by the pilots of JG 7, comprised two *Rotten* in which one wingman, positioned behind, monitored and guarded the *Rottenführer's* course. The two *Rotten* flew in a loose line abreast formation, but with the rear *Rotte* echeloned back so that effectively the wingman concept extended by *Rotte* to the whole *Schwarm*, and resulted in a 'finger-four' formation, broadly resembling the fingers of an outstretched hand.

centrifugal forces arising from banking ripped the belts. But these teething troubles were easily sorted out by a well-trained groundcrew.

Initially, it was foreseen that a Revi 16B reflector gunsight would be installed, a tried and tested type used by the Luftwaffe's fighter units for much of the war, although it was also planned to fit as many Me 262s as possible with the new EZ 42 gyroscopic sight. The latter would permit a pilot to fire at a target without allowance for the movement from fixed guns built into the longitudinal axis of the carrying aircraft. When approaching a target, a pilot had to ensure that he continuously twisted the range-finding button on the aircraft's control column so that the growing target was permanently encapsulated in the dial, as well as making sure that the cross-wire was contained within the target-circle on the target. The precise angle of deflection was obtained within two seconds. Accuracy could be guaranteed to within 15 per cent of the angle of deflection in the longitudinal direction of the enemy and ten per cent perpendicularly.

Despite lacking numbers, the appearance of the Me 262 gave those Luftwaffe pilots slated to fly the jet cause for both encouragement and trepidation: encouragement, because finally they had an aircraft with which they could power past and away from most Allied escort fighters to get to the bombers, but trepidation as a result of having to learn and master an entirely new form of propulsion capable of unprecedented speed and to turn the aircraft into an efficient tactical asset.

In the relatively brief period that Me 262s were operational, air combat tactics and formations were fluid, and varied between JG 7 and JV 44 as time progressed. JG 7's pilots tended to adopt the traditional Luftwaffe fighter flight element of the four-aircraft *Schwarm*, which was broken down into two sections of two-aircraft *Rotten* each comprised of a leader and a wingman flying slightly behind and above.

JV 44's tactics for attacking enemy bombers were greatly influenced by the low number of machines and pilots available for operations at any one time. It was quite usual for the *Jagdverband* to have just six serviceable jets operational, and wherever possible, with such low numbers, pilots tended to favour the deployment of their Me 262s in *Ketten* – the early-war, tried and tested element of three aircraft – as opposed to the *Schwarm*. The *Kette* was also preferred since, on most runways, it allowed three aircraft to take off, side-by-side. Once airborne in a *Kette*, the aircraft would be staggered below and/or behind each other, but rarely behind and above, since the unsatisfactory field of vision from the Me 262 precluded this. Respective *Ketten* would fly at 300m intervals.

As a result of the Me 262's lack of manoeuvrability, maintaining formations in elements larger than *Ketten* proved more difficult. Once visual contact was made with a bomber formation, one group was selected as the target and the jets would manoeuvre behind it so as to mount their attack from the rear. Getting into an effective attack position, however, at a range of about 1,000m on a dead-level approach was often challenging due to the great speed and turning radius of the Me 262. Thus, decisions regarding the attack had to be made quickly and at great distances from the target, from where it was difficult to correctly assess the bombers' range, course and altitude.

Furthermore, the very speed of the Me 262 – its greatest tactical advantage – curtailed the time available to a pilot to score hits on a target. Galland recalled:

The pilots of JV 44, including at least six Knight's Cross-holders, wait at readiness outside their operations hut at Munich-Riem in March 1945. Identifiable from left to right are Major Erich Hohagen (Knight's Cross, first left), Hauptmann Walter Krupinski (Knight's Cross, third from left), Oberst Günther Lützow (Knight's Cross, standing in leather overcoat), Oberst Johannes Steinhoff (Knight's Cross, seated centre), Oberleutnant Blomert (leaning against hut), Unteroffizier Eduard Schallmoser (standing in forage cap), Fahnenjunker-Oberfeldwebel Klaus Neumann (Knight's Cross, seated on arm of chair in forage cap) and Leutnant Heinz Sachsenberg (Knight's Cross, of the Fw 190D-9-equipped *Platzschutzschwarm*, standing in officer's cap). Note the field telephone linked to the operations room at Feldkirchen on the table ready to receive an 'Alarmstart' and flare pistols for firing start signals across the airfield to unit personnel. (Author's Collection)

My pilots were authorised to open fire from 600m. They were also permitted to fire a short burst before that if they noticed that they were being fired upon by the bombers. We also fired our R4M rockets at that range. We often hit two bombers with them in one go. The Me 262 could only count on success in attacking formations of heavy bombers if they were able to approach in fairly close formation, and not if they approached at great distances apart. The *Kette* had

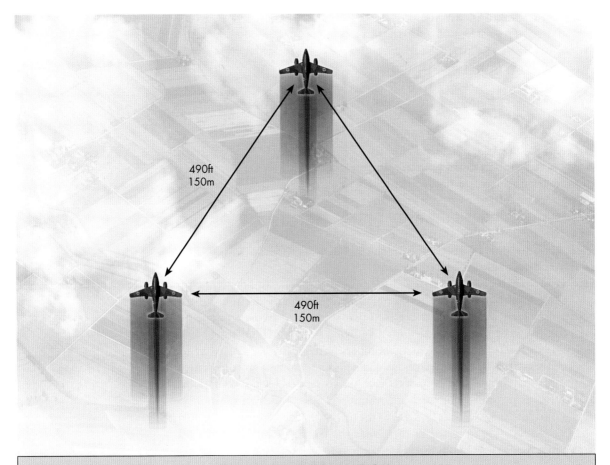

490ft
150m

490ft
150m

Me 262 *KETTE* FORMATION

In the case of the *Kette* formation, as favoured by the pilots of JV 44, once airborne, the aircraft would be staggered below and/or behind each other. *Ketten* would fly at 300m intervals. The pilots of JV 44 would also take off in elements of three, as runway widths at Munich-Riem allowed this.

to at least remain at one height; a clear-cut allocation of targets had to be made and the whole *Kette* had to fire simultaneously in order to make the defensive fire of the bombers disperse.

From 600m onwards, you had to fly in a perfectly straight line whilst starting your offensive fire. When you were 150m away at the latest, you had to turn away. You had to turn away above the bomber whatever happened; on no account could you afford to turn away from the bomber while still directly behind it, thus exposing your belly, as then it was almost certain that you would have been hit. But, if you had approached to within 200m, there was only one way out, and that was to turn away as close as possible, passing over the whole bomber formation. In any case, it was dangerous to turn away by flying underneath, as pieces of shot-down bombers, men bailing out, jettisoned bombs or burning aircraft flew straight into your face or into your turbines.

Manufactured by Deutsches Waffen und Munitions Fabrik, the R4M *Orkan* 55mm air-to-air rocket was an unrotated, rail or tube-launched, single venturi, solid fuel-propelled, multi-fin stabilised missile, with the warhead contained in an exceptionally thin one-millimetre sheet steel case enclosed in two pressed steel sections welded together and holding the Hexogen high-explosive charge. The missile bore a high charge weight to case weight ratio. The fuse was designed to discriminate between thin skin and main aircraft structure and to penetrate 60 to 100cm into a target aircraft before detonation to give maximum blast effect.

The R4M was to be launched from wooden underwing racks, mounted by four screws and positioned outside of the engines, with the connections between the launch rack and the wing surface faired in to counteract the possibility of air eddies as much as possible. The standard launch rack, known as the EG.-R4M, measured approximately 700mm in length, with each rocket being fitted with sliding lugs so that it could hang freely from the guide rails.

The wooden EG.-R4M launch rack with channels for 12 R4Ms fitted to the underside starboard wing of an Me 262A-1a of JG 7. With a rack weighing only 20kg, more than one could be carried beneath each wing, but as far as is known this never happened. (EN Archive)

Prior to loading into the rack, seven of the R4M's eight fins were held in a folded-down position by binding them with spring-steel wire made with spherical or similarly thickened ends. The rocket was pushed along the guiderail until the rear sliding lug was arrested by a notch in the rail. At the back of each rail was a terminal contact block connecting the ignition wires that hung down close to the socket. Once fired, the eighth fin was designed to spring free, which, in turn, released the binding wire, thus allowing the remaining seven fins to open – a process which commenced at about 400mm from the rail and finished once the rocket had flown approximately 2.5m.

Galland recounted:

On the Me 262 we could mount the R4M outside of the turbines under the wings, 12 on each side, with little aerodynamic disturbance. They were fired via a switch relay in 0.03 seconds of one another and aimed in exactly the same way as the MK 108, with a natural dispersion of about 35 square metres. But on account of the arrangement of the rockets, a shotgun-like pattern was made, creating a rectangle around the bomber. One hit – any hit – no matter where it was scored, sufficed to destroy a four-engined bomber. The loss of speed from the Me 262 as a result of mounting the R4M was insignificant. The projectiles were mounted with an upward inclination of eight degrees and fired at 600m, at which range they had the same ballistics as the MK 108. When you fired them, you just heard '*ssssshhhh*' – just a whisper.

Steinhoff recalled even greater range capability:

The great advantage of the rockets was that although their speed only slightly exceeded that of sound, they could be let off 1,100m away from the target – and from this range continued until they represented a field of fire of over 30m by 14m. This meant that by releasing all his rockets at once against a close formation of bombers,

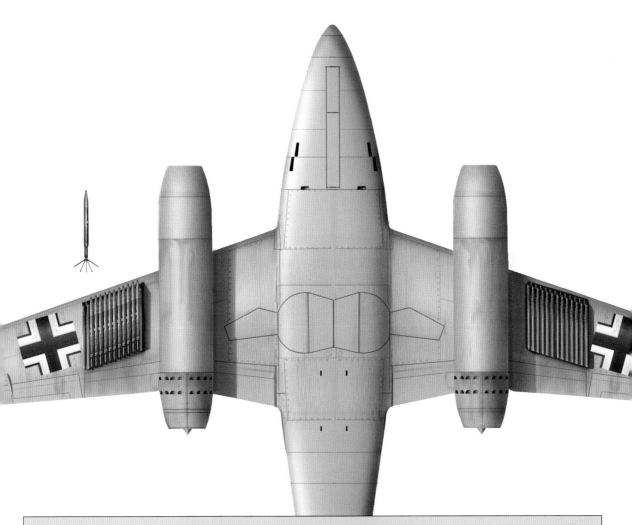

Me 262A-1a R4M ROCKET ARMAMENT

In addition to its nose-mounted 30mm cannon, the Me 262A-1a could be fitted with a pair of wooden EG.-R4M racks with channels for loading 12 R4M *Orkan* 55mm air-to-air rockets. Manufactured by a consortium led by the Deutsches Waffen und Munitions Fabrik, the R4M was a single venturi, solid fuel-propelled, multi-fin (there were eight fins) stabilised missile, with the warhead contained in an exceptionally thin one-millimetre sheet steel case enclosed in two pressed steel sections welded together and holding the Hexogen high-explosive charge. The missile bore a high charge weight to case weight ratio. The fuse was designed to discriminate between thin skin and main aircraft structure, and to penetrate 60–100cm into a target aircraft before detonation to give maximum blast effect.

The EG.-R4M rack measured approximately 700mm in length, with each rocket being fitted with sliding lugs so that it could hang freely from the guide rails. Each rocket was loaded from the rear of the rack, with its eighth fin held in place by the rail securing the wire binding. The rocket was pushed along the guide-rail until the rear sliding lug was arrested by a notch in the rail. At the back of each rail was a terminal contact block connecting the ignition wires which hung down close to the socket. Once fired, the eighth fin was designed to spring free, which, in turn, released the binding wire, thus allowing the remaining seven fins to open – a process which commenced at about 400mm from the rail and finished once the rocket had flown approximately 2.5m.

It was calculated that the loss of speed incurred by an Me 262 as a result of a launch rack being fitted was approximately 16km/h. The R4M had been expected to obtain an 80 per cent kill score at 500–600m.

a pilot couldn't miss. We had, at last, the means not only of combating these hitherto almost unassailable formations, but of destroying them. But – and it is a big 'but' – it was 'five minutes to twelve'; in other words early April before we got the rocket armament, and then only enough to equip a few aircraft.

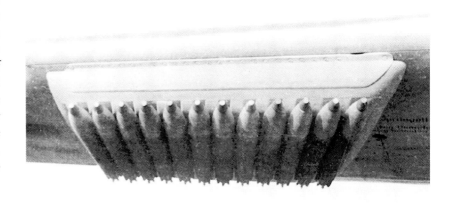

While there is no doubting the Me 262 was a superlative combat aircraft, its principal advantage – speed – could be neutralised if an Allied fighter pilot could force his German counterpart into a sudden, evasive hard turn. In so doing, speed would drain rapidly and the aircraft could become slow and unwieldy in manoeuvring at lower speeds. And yet, from the perspective of a P-51 pilot, successfully engaging an Me 262 in combat was a challenge. In one of III./JG 7's early encounters, on 21 February 1945, around 15 of the *Gruppe*'s Me 262s attacked P-51s of the USAAF's 479th Fighter Group (FG) near Potsdam. The Mustang pilots quickly recovered, turning into the jets, which broke away in a climb before returning for a second strike from above and to the rear. The American pilots involved reported:

A battery of 12 R4M 55mm air-to-air rockets loaded into their wooden launch rack beneath the starboard wing outboard of the engine nacelle of an Me 262 of JG 7. Prior to loading into the rack, seven of the rocket's eight fins were held in a folded-down position by binding them with spring-steel wire made with spherical or similarly thickened ends. The wire ends were then crossed and the eighth fin pressed down to hold the other seven in place. Each rocket was loaded from the rear of the rack, with the eighth fin held in place by the rail securing the wire binding. The rocket was pushed along the guide rail until the rear sliding lug was arrested by a notch in the rail. (EN Archive)

> . . . this kept up for three or four breaks, neither us nor Jerry being able to get close enough for a shot. Each time we would break they would climb straight ahead, outdistancing us. The Jerry pilots were aggressive and experienced. If caught in a turn they would roll out and climb away. It was impossible to catch or climb with them. Fighting took place from 12,000ft up to 26,000ft.
>
> A P-51 cannot climb with the jet, particularly if it has an initial altitude advantage. However, a P-51 can out-turn the jet. Red Flight out-turned the jets, having dropped their tanks just after being bounced. The jet was faster on a straight and level run. Its rate of roll was excellent, but its turning radius was poor. Their job seemed to have been to force us to drop our tanks so that we would have to leave. We were over southwest Berlin and we found the expenditure of gas while attempting to close very heavy. It was necessary to use full power all the time. The jets flew excellent formation and never allowed themselves to be caught in a bad position.

This encounter ended without loss to either side. Seven days later, on 28 February, the *Geschwader Stab* and III./JG 7 combined to send up 29 Me 262s from all three III. *Gruppe* airfields against a USAAF raid of more than 1,000 heavy bombers, escorted by nearly 700 fighters, attacking oil, armaments and transport targets across northern and central Germany. The jets engaged the B-17s of the 3rd Air Division in line astern from 6,000–7,000m between Braunschweig and Magdeburg just after 1015 hrs.

In their post-mission report, USAAF Intelligence Officers recorded:

Analysis of Me 262 tactics on 3 March reveals that the jets preferred to attack from either 6 or 12 o'clock. In most cases, attacks from other directions turned out to be feints. No preference was shown regarding the level of approach, but high approaches were generally not very high and low ones not very low. The number making a particular pass varied from one to four, but when more than one attacked, an echelon (almost in trail) formation was used. Breakaways varied considerably, although they always combined a change in altitude with a change in direction. Bomb groups were bounced while strung out in bombing formation and the jets completely ignored German flak while attacking.

The Me 262 pilots did not seem to be particular as to which group of the bomber column they attacked, and they were not averse to climbing back for a second pass after diving away from the first one. In some instances, the jets seemed to glide with power off when attacking, probably to obtain a longer firing burst by lessening the rate of closure.

Oberfeldwebel Hermann Buchner considered the Me 262 to have been 'years ahead of its time'. Having transitioned to the Messerschmitt interceptor from a ground-attack unit, Buchner proved himself a potent jet pilot, scoring several victories in the aircraft while with JG 7. He was awarded the Knight's Cross in July 1944 for 46 aerial victories – an extraordinary score for a ground-attack pilot. (Author's Collection, courtesy of Buchner)

Six *Viermots* had fallen to the guns of JG 7, and three escort fighters also became victims. Although the USAAF claimed six Me 262s shot down, such losses are not recorded on the German side.

Leutnant Hermann Buchner, who claimed 12 victories with the Me 262, served with 9./JG 7. He explained to the author:

The Me 262 reached us too late, although it was years ahead of its time from the point of view of its technology. Of course, there were shortcomings, but with more time and sufficient operational experience, these could have been eliminated. The main problem was that the crews had to work out new methods of attack and had to learn how to manage at such high speed.

In an attack, firing time was reduced – we reached the target ridiculously fast. I accounted for most of my claims by basically approaching from the rear. Of course, you had to fly through the escort. This was somewhat more difficult with the Fw 190, but was no problem with the Me 262. With a sufficient number of Me 262s deployed, the escort fighters had no chance of preventing a jet from making its attack.

An attack began at a distance of 500m; one had to overcome one's basic instincts and get through the defensive fire of the bomber. It was very important to make the target the tail-gunner's turret, just where you made out the muzzle flash and smoke of the machine guns. If the rear gunner had been taken out, success was much more certain. And when the R4M rocket was introduced, the successes were even better.

CHAPTER 6
COMBAT

25 July 1944 – the fighting in Normandy meant that Allied strategic air power was rendering support to American ground forces breaking out from the beachhead as part of Operation *Cobra*. In a massive 'carpet bombing' operation, 1,880 bombers of the USAAF's Eighth and Ninth Air Forces dropped 3,400 tons of bombs ahead of an American attack west of Saint-Lô, but some of this ordnance fell short, coming down amidst American units, inflicting 482 casualties among US forces.

Before the bombers came, waves of fighters from the Ninth Air Force targeted German positions along the Saint-Lô–Periers road at three-minute intervals. The Spitfires, Typhoons and Mustangs of the RAF's 2nd TAF were also busy across Normandy, mounting fighter patrols, ground-attack and reconnaissance missions. For the German defenders of France, it was nothing short of carnage.

Also that day, RAF Bomber Command sent Lancasters and Mosquitos to attack an airfield and signals depot at Saint-Cyr, while another force struck at V1 flying-bomb launch and storage sites. Over Austria, the USAAF's strategic bombing effort fell upon Linz as B-17s and B-24s of the Fifteenth Air Force bombed a tank factory there, as well as a marshalling yard at Villach. In Italy, tactical bombers of the Twelfth Air Force struck bridges in the northwest of the country, as well as railway lines, storage dumps and communications lines through the Po River valley. Finally, in Poland, American fighters attacked Mielec airfield as part of a long-range 'Frantic' shuttle mission. As the US fighters approached their landing fields in the Soviet Union, P-51s managed to shoot down several Ju 87 ground-attack aircraft from a large formation as they returned from a mission in the east.

Supplementing this relentless air assault on Hitler's 'Fortress Europe' were the Mosquito photo-reconnaissance aircraft of No 544 Sqn based at Benson, in Oxfordshire. For several months the unit had been providing photographic cover of western Europe, Norway, southern France, southern Germany and Austria, and on 25 July it mounted eight single-aircraft sorties to targets in

Belgium, the Netherlands, northern and central Germany and northern and southwest France. The last sortie for that day was carried out by Flt Lt A. E. Wall and his navigator, Flg Off A. S. Lobban, when their Mosquito PR XVI took off from Benson at 1655 hrs. The crew had been briefed to cover Stuttgart, Neuburg, Fürstenfeldbruck and Munich, in southern Germany.

The Mosquito PR XVI was the RAF's main long-range, high-altitude photo-reconnaissance aircraft, fitted with a pressure cabin and powered by a pair of Rolls-Royce Merlin 72/73 engines that gave it a maximum speed of 415mph and a range of 2,450 nautical miles. Although unarmed, it was a fast and potent machine for this type of mission.

By early evening Wall and Lobban had reached Munich and were circling the city for oblique shots at a height of 30,000ft. As Wall banked the Mosquito to port, Lobban spotted a twin-engined enemy fighter 400 yards astern that tracked the British aircraft and also banked to port. This was an Me 262, flown most probably by Leutnant Alfred Schreiber of EKdo 262 based at Lechfeld, some 80km west of Munich. Lobban shouted a warning to Wall and the pilot opened up to full boost and revs, attaining a speed of 200 ASI (approximately 327mph true airspeed), which was increased to 260 ASI (412mph true airspeed) by diving to 28,000ft. At this, the German pilot banked again sharply in order to get a good look at his quarry, before turning away to port. There then followed a six-phase 'cat-and-mouse' game between the jet interceptor and the Mosquito.

From a range of 1,800m, the Me 262 closed in from dead astern to 900m. Wall turned to port, but realised that the jet would be able to come out of the sun and so he straightened out. The German pilot opened fire with his MK 108 cannon from around 700m, but missed his target. Wall again turned to port and climbed slowly at 380mph true airspeed. Although the Me 262 followed easily, the Mosquito was able to keep inside the jet's turning circle. It then broke away to the north, while the Mosquito turned south.

Handicapped by the width of his turn whilst flying at an altitude of 9,500m, the Me 262 pilot positioned himself on the tail of the British aircraft and opened fire again from 730m. Again, the cannon shells were wide of their target. Wall made another fast, tight turn to port, pursued by the Me 262, which attempted to turn inside the Mosquito but failed. After a complete circle, the jet broke away in the opposite direction to the Mosquito.

However, the German pilot was undeterred, and after making a wide turn he again manoeuvred onto the tail of the PR XVI before engaging it with a third burst of cannon fire. Wall repeated his turning process and the Me 262 again attempted to follow. The two aircraft made three complete turns, the Mosquito always tighter. At one point the tables were turned, and Wall found himself on the tail of the jet and in a favourable position to fire had his Mosquito been armed. By this stage, both aircraft were losing altitude. The Mosquito broke off south towards the cloud-layered Bavarian Alps while the Me 262 headed north.

Moments later, after repeating a wide turn to the north, the jet was back on the Mosquito's tail, making a shallow dive to disappear below. This time Wall turned sharply to port at 373mph true airspeed, pulling hard back on the stick. As their aircraft turned, the crew heard two 'dull thuds' on the underside of the Mosquito. The Me 262 was out of sight and Lobban attempted to open the emergency exit in preparation for bailing out if necessary. Despite the concern, Wall pressed on to the south, heading for the mountains and cloud cover, using full boost and revs.

Leutnant Alfred Schreiber of EKdo 262 may well have attempted to shoot down the Mosquito PR XVI crewed by Flt Lt A. E. Wall and Flg Off A. S. Lobban of No 544 Sqn over southern Germany on 25 July 1944. 'Bubi' Schreiber later joined the newly-formed 9./JG 7, and he was killed on 26 November 1944 when his Me 262 crashed. (EN Archive)

While over the Austrian Tyrol at 27,000ft, the jet was seen again at 3,000 yards dead astern. The Mosquito went into a dive and weaved. The Me 262 passed by, but comparatively slowly as the Mosquito reached the cover of cloud at 15,000ft. On emerging into clear sky, the Me 262 was seen to be 800 yards behind, still in pursuit, but it did not open fire. Wall made for another long bank of cloud, with the German jet having closed to 450 yards by the time the cloud was reached. The Mosquito was in the cloud for three to four minutes at 14,000ft. As it emerged, the Me 262 had disappeared. Wall climbed to 24,000ft, and using escape maps set course for Italy, seeing Venice a short while later 30 miles ahead. The Mosquito eventually landed at No. 544 Sqn's forward operational base at Fermo, on the Adriatic coast, three-and-a-half hours after leaving Benson.

Wall had displayed considerable skill in turning south each time he broke away from the Me 262, believing, quite correctly, that the enemy machine had a fairly short endurance, and that by doing so he could pull it away from its base. Leutnant Schreiber subsequently claimed – mistakenly – the Mosquito as destroyed for the first 'kill' to be credited to EKdo 262.

Importantly, Wg Cdr G. E. F. Proctor of the Air Ministry Branch's A.I.2(g) intelligence section noted in his post-mission report that:

At times it appeared that the high speed of the enemy aircraft was a disadvantage in that it rapidly overshot when coming up from astern, and had to make a wide turn in order to retrieve its position. The fact that it could make a wide turn, travelling in the opposite direction of the Mosquito to do so, and still got into position again gives some idea of its superior speed.

In this first encounter between an Allied aircraft and the Me 262, Proctor had accurately highlighted the jet's positives (especially when set against an aircraft

This USAAF intelligence diagram portrayed the Me 262 as a 'triple-threat' aircraft and a 'troublesome customer', able to deploy hit-and-run strikes to combat fighter escorts and use its great speed when attacking bombers, while also operating as a bomber at either medium heights in daylight or at low-level at dusk. According to this diagram, 'Allied troops called it "the silent strafer" because it streaked past with little sound'. (Author's Collection)

AGAINST FIGHTER ESCORT
ME-262 USES HIT-AND-RUN TACTICS

AGAINST BOMBERS
ME-262 DIVES THROUGH FORMATION AT GREAT SPEED

ME-262'S AS BOMBERS
ATTACK IN PAIRS AT 6,000 FEET

AT DUSK, WHEN VISIBILITY IS POOR, ME-262 COMES IN AT 1,000 FT., DIVES TO 500 FT., TO RELEASE BOMBS

TRIPLE-THREAT TACTICS made the ME-262 a troublesome customer. Carrying at least four 30-millimeter cannons in its nose and two 551-pound bombs under its fuselage, it was adapted to low-level bombing and strafing of Allied installations behind the lines as well as to lightning strikes at our bomber formations. Its heavy armor—15 millimeters thick in some places—enabled it to tangle with our fighters if necessary. When carrying bombs, it was slowed down so much that it sometimes took along its own fighter escort. Allied troops called it "the silent strafer" because it streaked past with little sound.

as fast as the Mosquito) and its negatives (its wide turn) – factors that would become very pertinent in the combats that would take place over Germany the following year.

Just over six months later, the Third Reich's war predicament on the Western Front had deteriorated considerably. In early February the Allies prepared to drive on the Rhine: their advance would be across a front of 400km, from the Swiss border, across eastern France, Luxembourg, Belgium and into the Netherlands. In the north, the forces of Maj Gen Omar Bradley and Field Marshal Sir Bernard Montgomery would mount a series of assaults on the great river and attempt exploitation of the weakening German defences. The commander of the US Army's 82nd Airborne Division, Lt Gen James M. Gavin, noted in his diary on 3 February 1945, 'The Germans appear to be beaten, and beaten badly'.

By this time JG 7 was still in the process of preparing for operations, and the Luftwaffe had only managed to get one *Geschwader*, KG 51, to deploy the Me 262 to any meaningful extent – and not as interceptors, but in the role which Hitler had craved, as bombers. From their bases at Rheine, Hopsten, Hesepe, Achmer and Essen-Mühlheim, the Me 262A-2as of I. and II./KG 51 under Major Heinz Unrau

and Hauptmann Hans-Joachim Grundmann, respectively, carried out strikes against Allied troop concentrations, supply dumps and traffic, as well as bridges. While the attacks were determined, regular and usually effective, they were, in reality, little more than pinpricks for the Allied ground forces. Furthermore, the former bomber pilots who flew the high-speed jets found air combat against Allied fighters a real challenge, while Allied pilots seemed to have little to fear, as is testified in their combat reports from this time.

On 14 February British and Canadian forces approached the south bank of the Rhine opposite the fortified town of Kleve, leading KG 51 to fly a total of 55 sorties against Allied ground targets in the area during the day. Between 0755 and 0916 hrs, 13 aircraft from II./KG 51 were sent from Rheine and Essen-Mühlheim to attack enemy troop assemblies in the area. Having dropped their containers of fragmentation bombs over the targets, the jets turned for home, flying low at just over 900m. But, in a typical such encounter, between Enschede and Coesfeld, two of them were spotted by Flt Lt Lyall C. Shaver who was leading Red Section in a formation of Typhoons from No 439 Sqn RCAF which were reforming after conducting an armed reconnaissance of the area that morning. He subsequently noted in his Combat Report:

Aside from its envisaged role as an interceptor, the Me 262 was also deployed by KG 51 as a high-speed, hit-and-run fighter-bomber on the Western Front in the second half of 1944. The jets targeted Allied transport, armoured columns, troop assemblies and bridges, usually dropping 250 or 500kg bombs or bomb containers loaded with two-kilogramme fragmentation bombs. Here, Me 262A-1a Wk-Nr. 110813, which was built at Leipheim as a standard interceptor, has been fitted with racks for bomb-dropping trials in late 1944 and is loaded with two 500kg SC 500 weapons. The cable from a generator cart is plugged into the aircraft to charge its battery. This jet was used for training purposes by III./EJG 2 later in 1944, and in 1945 it is believed to have been assigned to JG 7. (EN Archive)

> While flying west at 7,000ft approximately 20 miles from Coesfeld, I observed two Me 262s line abreast flying west at 3,000ft. I informed the other pilots and dove to attack.

Red 3, Flg Off A. H. (Hugh) Fraser, heard Shaver's call over the R/T and followed his section leader down towards the Me 262s, which were flying straight and level. The Typhoons came in directly from behind and slightly below the jets. Shaver took the one on their right and fired a two-second burst from 100 yards, but saw no strikes:

> I raised my sights slightly, closed to 50 yards and again opened fire with a two-second burst. The enemy aircraft exploded in mid-air. I flew through the blast of the exploded aircraft and saw the other Me 262 break off to port. I fired two two-second bursts from quarter position, but did not observe any strikes.

Taken from a wartime intelligence manual, two gun camera stills captured by a P-51 show an Me 262 seconds after taking hits from the Mustang's guns during operations over the Reich on 22 February 1945 at the opening of Operation *Clarion*, a major air offensive aimed at the German transport and communications network. The Messerschmitt's port Jumo 004 has caught fire. (Author's Collection)

This Me-262 is on the receiving end of an Eighth Air Force mission. The jet was claimed destroyed, the pilot P-51's strikes, in gun camera photos from 22 February bailed out after his port propulsion unit was set afire.

I then saw Red 3 (F/O Fraser) attacking from above and to the rear of the second enemy aircraft.

Fraser fired a three-second burst at his target from 400 yards and closed to 50 yards, but the jet disappeared into cloud. Fraser continued his pursuit and went beneath the cloud:

> I saw the port engine fall off the Me 262. I pulled up to 1,500ft under cloud and saw the enemy aircraft hit the ground and burst into flames. I climbed to 8,000ft, and during the climb passed a parachute which had something burning at the end, but I don't think it was the pilot.

As Shaver passed overhead, he 'observed a plume of black smoke bulging above cloud'. Subsequently, Flt Lt Lyall C. Shaver and Flg Off Hugh Fraser claimed two Me 262s shot down after bouncing the jets. Both German pilots were killed over Rosendahl-Osterwick. They were Oberleutnant Hans-Georg Richter and Feldwebel Werner Witzmann of 5./KG 51.

Exactly a week later, in the late afternoon of the 21st, Oberfeldwebel Hermann Wieczorek of 2./KG 51 flew a bombing mission to targets in the Kleve area. His Me 262 was hit by Allied anti-aircraft fire while over the target, and after dropping his ordnance he turned to head back to Hopsten. Only minutes later, however, as he crossed the Rhine and passed north of the town of Emmerich at around 2,500m, he suddenly found himself confronted directly ahead by Spitfire IXs of No 412 Sqn RCAF on their way home from an armed reconnaissance in the Munster area. Wieczorek put his Me 262 into a shallow dive, but as he did so Flt Lt I. A. Stewart, flying in Yellow Section, spotted him.

> I was able to get approximately a two- to three-second burst at him with 20–30 degrees deflection before he passed under me. I did not see strikes on him during the burst, but when I broke around after him there was black smoke coming out of his starboard engine nacelle. The enemy aircraft was last observed diving down, going northeast and omitting smoke.

Stewart registered a claim for one Me 262 damaged, but Wieczorek was able to make it back to Hopsten, where he landed safely at 1753 hrs. Although this may seem an inconsequential encounter, it actually demonstrates how, even with a damaged turbo unit, an Me 262 could use its speed to escape and survive when pursued by fast piston-engined fighters.

But this did not always work, as was evidenced the following day when 19 Me 262s from KG 51 attacked American troop concentrations around Inden, Aldenoven and Geilenkirchen. One of the jets was flown by Wieczorek's comrade in 2. *Staffel*, Leutnant Kurt Piehl, who departed Hopsten late that afternoon carrying two SD 250 fragmentation bomb containers with which to attack an enemy column on the road from Düren to Pier, after which he was to make strafing runs.

1Lt Oliven T. Cowan of the 365th FG watches from the cockpit of his P-47 as his chief mechanic carefully paints an Me 262 'kill' marking just below the cockpit. It marked Cowan's shooting down of Leutnant Kurt Piehl of 2./KG 51 on 22 February 1945. (Author's Collection, courtesy of Cowan)

Unfortunately for Piehl, P-47s from the Ninth Air Force's 365th FG were on patrol in the area when they were alerted to the presence of the enemy jets. Leading a flight of Thunderbolts from the 388th Fighter Squadron (FS) was 1Lt Oliven T. Cowan, whose pilots saw the German jets strafing as they approached Düren. Piehl had just completed his attack, and was climbing in a banking turn to head back to Hopsten. Cowan reported:

After evading intense concentrations of our own flak, we had him below us. 'Red Flight' was at about 7,000–8,000ft when it made contact. The jet started to climb, but 'Elwood Red Leader' had altitude and headed him off. My flight at 11,000ft worked east so as to intercept him as he started for home. Soon, the jet began to head east towards home, while two members of 'Red Flight' were chasing and firing at him.

The jet was pulling away from them, but he didn't seem to want to turn and he couldn't dive too steeply. He appeared to want to climb but we already had altitude on him. When the jet started to pull away from 'Red Flight', I took my number two, leaving three and four as top cover, and started down. I pushed everything forward and went down with water injection. At approximately 5,000ft we were doing 530mph.

2Lt Thomas N. Threlkeld was flying as wingman to Cowan:

I was flying 'Elwood White Two' position when our squadron encountered Me 262s strafing on the deck. One of them tried to climb through us but was turned back down by 'Red Flight'. At this time, I was on Lt Cowan's wing at about 11,000ft. We went into a dive, and with the altitude advantage and a little water injection, my leader pulled up on his tail and fired a burst from his guns. Then it was my turn.

I do not believe the jet pilot saw me until too late. I shallowed my dive, pulled my nose through and gave him a burst from my guns. He then dropped out of my sights at 300ft altitude. I lowered my nose and saw him crash into the ground. When he crashed, I observed a puff of black smoke but no flame. After the smoke drifted away I could see small pieces of wreckage of the jet plane scattered over a

Hauptmann Heinz Gutmann was typical of the experienced former bomber pilots who underwent conversion training for the Me 262. Awarded the Knight's Cross on 5 April 1944 while a pilot with He 111-equipped I./KG 53, he volunteered for fighter training after disbandment of his *Gruppe* in August 1944. Having completed a course on the Me 262 with III./EJG 2 at Lechfeld in late 1944, Gutmann was posted to III./JG 7 on 9 December. He was appointed *Staffelkapitän* of 9. *Staffel* in February 1945, but was shot down and killed on 3 March after claiming an enemy bomber. His comrade, Hermann Buchner, recalled, 'I think he might have been killed outright as he did not attempt to bail out'. (EN Archive)

wide area, as though it had exploded on impact. One important factor was the advantage of altitude over the jet, which we could use to gain enough speed to overtake that aircraft.

Piehl had hit the ground northwest of Düren. His loss was the 175th victory for the 365th FG.

The Me 262 interceptor units fought a different kind of war at altitude, high over the Reich, always attempting to use their speed to slice through the USAAF fighter escort screen to get to the bombers. On 3 March 1945, for example, the *Geschwader Stab* and III./JG 7 combined to send up 29 Me 262s from all three III. *Gruppe* airfields against more than 1,000 heavy bombers, and nearly 700 escort fighters, targeting oil, armaments and transport targets across northern and central Germany. The jets attacked the B-17s of the 3rd Air Division in line astern from 6,000–7,000m between Braunschweig and Magdeburg just after 1015 hrs.

Hauptmann Heinz Gutmann, a former bomber pilot with III./KG 53 and a Knight's Cross-holder now flying with 10./JG 7, Leutnant Karl Schnörrer of 11./JG 7 and a veteran of *Kommando Nowotny*, and Oberfeldwebel Helmut Lennartz of 9./JG 7 each claimed one Flying Fortress destroyed, while Oberfähnrich Heinz Russel of 9./JG 7 and Oberfeldwebel Hermann Buchner managed to shoot down a P-47 and a P-51, respectively, with Buchner also claiming a B-17. The latter recalled:

We broke through the fighter escorts but then found ourselves under massive defensive fire from the bombers' turret gunners. When we were about 1,000m from the bombers, Gutmann's cockpit flashed with fire and his fighter sheared away from our formation and dived away vertically. I think he might have been killed outright, as he did not attempt to bail out.

Gutmann's Me 262 hit the ground a few kilometres south of Braunschweig, but six *Viermots* fell to the guns of JG 7 and three escort fighters were also shot down. Although the USAAF claimed six jets, such losses are not recorded on the German side. USAAF Intelligence Officers provided a detailed analysis of jet tactics based on the post-mission reports from the aircrews:

Analysis of Me 262 tactics on 3 March reveals that the jets preferred to attack from either 6 or 12 o'clock. In most cases, attacks from other directions turned out to be feints. No preference was shown regarding the level of approach, but high approaches were generally not very high and low ones not very low. The number making a particular pass varied from one to four, but when more than one attacked, an echelon (almost in trail) formation was used. Breakaways varied considerably, although they always combined a change in altitude with a change in direction. Bomb groups were bounced while strung out in bombing formation, and the jets completely ignored German flak while attacking.

The Me 262 pilots did not seem to be particular as to which group of the bomber column they attacked, and they were not averse to climbing back for a

second pass after diving away from the first one. In some instances, the jets seemed to glide with power off when attacking, probably to obtain a longer firing burst by lessening the rate of closure.

On 18 March nearly 1,200 US heavy bombers attacked railway and armaments factories in the Berlin area. They were escorted by 426 fighters. 9./JG 7 put up six aircraft, each fitted with two underwing batteries of 12 of the new R4M rockets. The jets intercepted the *Viermots* over Rathenow, and a total of 144 rockets was fired into the American formation from distances of between 400–600m. Pilots reported astonishing amounts of resulting debris and aluminium fragments – pieces of wing, engines and cockpits flying through the air from aircraft hit by the missiles.

Oberfähnrich Walter Windisch, who had two victories to his credit by the time he joined JG 7 from JG 52, was one of the first pilots of the *Geschwader* to experience the effect of the R4M in operational conditions:

Flying the Me 262 was like a kind of 'life insurance'. But I was on that first sortie on 18 March during which R4M rockets were used and I experienced something beyond my conception. The destructive effect against the targets was immense. It almost gave me a feeling of being invincible. However, the launching grids for the rockets were not of optimum design – they were still too rough and ready – and compared with conventionally powered aircraft, when you went into a turn with the Me 262, flying became a lot more difficult because the trimming was not too good.

In total I. and III./JG 7 had deployed 37 aircraft, of which 13 engaged, with two pilots reporting probable victories, and there were six *Herausschüsse* – incidents of bombers being 'cut out' and forced away from their formations. The *Geschwader* suffered the loss of three pilots, with another badly wounded, while five jets had to be written off due to severe battle damage, with a further two requiring repair. Nevertheless, the 18th was the first real indication of what

Me 262A-1a 'Green 3' of the *Geschwaderstab* of JG 7 at Brandenburg-Briest in early 1945. The aircraft is finished in a relatively rare application of streaked horizontal lines and has been fitted with a pair of 21cm W.Gr.21 air-to-air mortar tubes visible beneath the fuselage aft of the nosewheel. These weapons were rarely fitted to the Me 262, but were used in trials in small numbers against USAAF bombers with a view to dispersing formations. (EN Archive)

Me 262A-1a 'White 7' of III./JG 7 fitted with a wooden EG.-R4M underwing launch rack and 12 DWM 55mm R4M Orkan air-to-air rockets beneath each wing. The *Geschwader* emblem has been applied to the aircraft's nose. (EN Archive)

impact a small, determined force of jet fighters could have upon the enemy – even allowing for poor operating conditions. USAAF Intelligence later graphically recorded:

> The jets launched their attacks from out of contrails and aggressively pressed home against the last two groups, in one instance to within 50 yards. Several concentrated attacks were made by two or four jets – others attacked singly. Jets made skilful use of superior speed, and although escort fighters engaged, only one jet was claimed damaged. Some 12–15 Me 262s made strong attacks on the 3rd Division from west of Salzwedel to Berlin; attacks, although not continuous, were skilful and aggressive, contrail being used to good effect; six bombers were lost to this attack.

Initial attack, about 20 minutes before the target, was on the low squadron of the second group in the column, which at the time was strung out and in poor formation. Four Me 262s in a formation similar to that used by P-51s came out of clouds and contrails from 5 o'clock low, closing to between 75 yards and point-blank range; three bombers were badly damaged in this attack. The second attack, by three Me 262s, came in from 6:30 to 7 o'clock, low to level, resulting in the entire tail section of one B-17 being shot off.

Windisch, like many of his contemporaries, was astonished at the capability of the Me 262:

> I considered it an honour to have been selected to fly it. Comparing it to other aircraft was like comparing a Formula One racing car to a truck. Apart from the take-off and landing phases, flying the Me 262 gave me a feeling of being far superior to all others. It also gave me a feeling of safety I had never expected, and which I had never experienced when flying the Me 109 – an increase in the probability of survival many times over.

The Allied strategic air forces returned on 21 March: this time nearly 1,300 bombers from the Eighth Air Force targeted 12 airfields across northwest Germany in another attempt to inflict damage on the jet fighter infrastructure – 107 B-17s of the 3rd Air Division also went to Plauen to bomb an armoured vehicle factory. With them came 750 P-51 escort fighters, including Mustangs of the 78th FG. Flying in 'Cargo Blue Flight' of the Group's 83rd FS that day was Capt Edwin H. Miller, who, at around 0945 hrs, saw an Me 262 attacking the bombers through thin cloud over the Wittenberg area. Miller's After Action Report illustrates well the typical tactics of an Me 262, and the fine balance pilots had to try to achieve between the jet's high speed versus its poor rate of turn:

> We saw two B-17s explode from this pass, and by the time we got to the bombers the jet had come around for a second pass and was firing on the formation as

my wingman [2Lt Robert F. Rohm] and I took pursuit. This was at 19,000ft. The jet then broke off his attack from the formation and went after a ship previously damaged. As the jet fired on this cripple, I fired a burst from about 2,000 yards to attempt to scare him away. I observed a few hits and the jet broke away and down in a dive to the left. I followed the jet in his dive and started to close slowly when I saw he was headed in a shallow dive for the clouds. My speed at this time was approximately 500mph. The 'Hun' went into the clouds and I followed because I was still closing and thought I could catch him. The overcast was thin, and as I broke out under it, I observed and identified the ship as an Me 262. He was in a turn to the left and I was able to cut him off and close more rapidly. He then straightened out and I closed on him, firing from about 500 to 100 yards, observing hits all over the ship. Pieces flew past

as a result of this attack. I then closed very rapidly. We were getting closer to the ground every second when I fired my last burst and 'clobbered' him good. I started to overrun him, pulling off to the left just as he went straight into the ground, exploding and smearing flame and debris all over. The pilot did not get out.

The Me 262 of Oberfeldwebel Helmut Recker of 10./EJG 2 is caught by the gun camera on the P-51 flown by 2Lt John Cunnick of the 38th FS/55th FG over Lechfeld airfield on 22 March 1945 as the latter rolled his fighter sharply and dived down towards the jet's cockpit, 'firing all the time'. Recker crashed at the southern edge of the airfield and was killed. (Author's Collection, courtesy of Gray)

The identity of Miller's victim cannot be determined with any certainty.

On 5 March the *Gruppenstab* of I./JG 7 had welcomed a new, very potent pilot to its ranks in the form of Oberleutnant Walter Schuck, a recipient of the Knight's Cross with Oakleaves with 198 victories to his credit scored while with JG 5 in the Far North. Shortly before midday on 24 March, four days after his first flight in an Me 262, Schuck and his wingman spotted 'three black dots' approximately 120km southwest of Berlin in the Leipzig–Dresden area. These comprised a USAAF F-5 reconnaissance aircraft, escorted by two P-51s.

At full speed, Schuck and his wingman came in behind the three American aircraft and opened fire. Schuck's wingman shot down the F-5, but the Mustang pilots made every attempt to avoid their jet-powered assailants by rolling, swerving and diving. Doggedly, Schuck stayed with them and eventually chose an opportune moment to fire at each. The first P-51 blew apart in the air at 1200 hrs, while five minutes later a wing broke away from the second fighter, which then nosed earthwards.

Throughout the spring of 1945, the Eighth, Twelfth and Fifteenth Air Forces prosecuted a relentless bombing campaign against aircraft and tank factories, oil refineries, railways, road junctions, ammunition dumps and bridges across southern Germany, Austria and Czechoslovakia. Against this onslaught was pitted the small number of Me 262s of JV 44 that arrived at Munich-Riem at the end of March.

One of the first known combats involving the unit took place on 2 April when the veteran fighter ace Hauptmann Walter Krupinski took off from Riem *immediately* after he had received his introduction to the Me 262 from Steinhoff (see Chapter 3). Climbing into the sky over Munich, Krupinski headed south towards the Bavarian Alps, and as he crossed the Tegernsee a message

came over the radio from the controller at Feldkirchen warning of enemy aircraft, identified as P-38 Lightnings, approaching from Innsbruck. He was ordered to return, but Krupinski chose to press on.

As he approached the city he spotted the distinctive twin-boom shape of the American long-range escort fighters of the Fifteenth Air Force. He closed in at 900km/h, hoping to claim a P-38 on his first flight in the Me 262. A pursuit ensued over the rooftops of Innsbruck with Krupinski on the tail of one of the Lightnings. He opened fire with his MK 108s, but his efforts were in vain and he watched in dismay as the P-38 slipped away beneath him. The Me 262 powered forward – too fast:

Know your enemy. Flt Off Ralf Delgado of the 354th FG points to the jet engine of an Me 262 on a USAAF three-view recognition poster. He is also holding a small model of a P-51 in his right hand, and is probably advising his colleague to aim for the jet's engines when making an attack. Delgado was credited with the destruction of an Me 262 of I./KG(J) 54 over Giebelstadt on 2 March 1945. (EN Archive)

> It was just the same as in the early days against the Russians when they flew those old biplanes, like the I-153, and the I-16 *Ratas* and we flew the Bf 109; there was such a difference in speed and you had to compensate – and on that occasion, I didn't.

As he touched down back at Riem, Krupinski still struggled to master the speed of the jet and he was forced to roll off the runway. Nevertheless, as he later informed Steinhoff, it was his opinion that in the Me 262, the Luftwaffe had the machine with which to fight back against the Allies.

P-38s of the Fifteenth Air Force would be the target again two days later, but once more the encounter would provide a salutary lesson. At 1100 hrs on 4 April, Leutnant Gottfried Fährmann and Unteroffizier Eduard Schallmoser took off from Riem to engage a formation of 12 Lightnings approaching Munich. As the jets closed in, head-on, at an altitude of just under 10,000m, Schallmoser attempted to open fire, but his four 30mm cannon remained frustratingly silent. He cursed and momentarily looked down to his control column, whereupon he realised that he had not correctly flipped away the safety guard over the firing button. It was a fateful distraction. Looking up

Me 262A-1a Wk-Nr. 111745 'White 5' of JV 44 seen parked in the unit's 'start area' at Munich-Riem. It was one of a number operated by the unit which were finished typically in a very plain application, probably of Dunkelgrün 83, on their fuselages and uppersurfaces, with Blue-Grey 76 on the undersides. This aircraft was flown by several pilots of the unit, including Unteroffiziere Eduard Schallmoser and Johann-Karl Müller. (Author's Collection)

again, to his horror, Schallmoser realised that he was on a collision course with one of the Lightnings, and desperately attempted to veer away, but to no avail. At an incredibly high closing speed, the Me 262 'grazed' the P-38's tail unit with the tip of its starboard wing.

In seconds however, he managed to form up with Fährmann and, somewhat shaken, returned to Riem. As he banked away, Schallmoser caught sight of the P-38 spiralling towards the ground and its pilot bailing out. Although his Me 262 had sustained only minor damage, the encounter came as another warning to the less experienced pilots of JV 44 to be very aware of the extreme speed of the jet.

Eight days later, during the early afternoon of 10 April, to the north, as described in Chapter 1, the Eighth Air Force struck at the jet units' airfields on a major scale. By this time in command of 3./JG 7, Oberleutnant Walter Schuck led seven Me 262s and achieved the impressive distinction of shooting down four B-17s within eight minutes over Oranienburg for his 203rd to 206th victories. Schuck and his group of jets were at 8,000m when they were directed towards the bombers, which were reported approaching from the northwest. To avoid the P-51 escort, Schuck brought his formation into attack on a zig-zag course at 10,000m, curving behind the enemy formation. But in doing so, he deployed a special tactic for attacking such an enormous 'armada'.

Oberleutnant Walter Schuck, far left, jokes with fellow pilots of JG 5 in the Far North in June 1944. Three months later, Schuck was awarded the Knight's Cross with Oakleaves to mark his 171 victories. He moved to JG 7 in early March 1945 and assumed command of 3. *Staffel* at Kaltenkirchen on the 26th of that month. Schuck is seen here with three other centurions (and Knight's Cross holders), and between them they would amass a total of 568 Arctic victories while serving with JG 5. They are, from the left, Walter Schuck, Franz Dörr, Heinrich Ehrler (who also subsequently served with JG 7) and Jakob Norz. (EN Archive)

A formation of hundreds of American four-engined bombers, even when flying in close formation, stretched for several kilometres through the sky from the lead squadron in the lead combat 'box' in the lead wing to the second flight in the last squadron in the rearmost 'box'. In order to reduce the danger of massed defensive fire from the hundreds of 0.50-cal. Browning machine guns the bombers carried in their various turrets, as well as to conserve fuel, it made sense to try to minimise the number of attacks undertaken, but in doing so, to maximise the effect of any single attack. Schuck described his method:

I would 'surf-ride' along the length of the bomber stream and then dive on the enemy from a height of 1,000m above. Selecting a bomber flying out on one of the flanks, I would put a short burst of fire into an inboard engine and then pull up and away while still at least 200m above the bomber in order to ensure safe recovery, climbing back up to 1,000m before repeating the process. Even though a 'ride' of this kind above the bombers took up several kilometres, such was the length of the average stream that it was usually possible to achieve multiple successes in the course of one roller-coaster pass.

The speed of the Me 262, in such a situation, when presented with such a large potential target, was also a great benefit.

With the sight of bombs raining down on Oranienburg below, Schuck fired his four MK 108s at a B-17 from 300m. A wing immediately disintegrated as the German ace flew towards another *Viermot*. His second target,

B-17G 44-8427 *HENN'S REVENGE* of the 303rd BG, took hits in its elevator and the crew bailed out of the spiralling aircraft. Schuck had to pull up sharply to avoid colliding with his victim. Soon afterwards, another bomber took the full force of the Me 262's four cannon in one wing; it veered over on its side and fell towards the earth trailing flames. Schuck then 'knocked down' a fourth Flying Fortress, this time B-17G 43-38606 *Moonlight Mission* of the 457th BG. Again, one of the B-17's inboard engines was hit and the wing sheared away. Schuck observed the crew escape the aircraft before it blew up at 5,000m.

At that moment, Schuck's aircraft was fired at by a P-51 and hit in the left Jumo engine. His instruments told him he was at an altitude of 8,200m and that power was failing. Mindful of his dwindling fuel supply, Schuck broke away and made course for Jüterbog airfield, although he was uncertain whether the runway there would be intact. With his engine trailing smoke, and chased by a pair of Mustangs, he decided to bail out at 300m between Brandenburg-Briest and Jüterbog. Schuck came down safely and was picked up by a baker on a bicycle, with whom he rode to the refuge of a nearby mill, where he was offered a cup of coffee.

A subsequent German radio message was intercepted which stated (a little inaccurately), 'Oblt. Schuck bailed out near Buschkuhnsdorf, near Holzdorf in the Scheinitz district. Successes: 1 Mustang and 2 Boeings. Attacked by 20 Mustangs. Engine caught fire and fuselage shot up. Is with his *Staffel*'.

The Flying Fortresses of the 3rd Air Division targeting Brandenburg-Briest were also attacked by approximately ten jets, but in this case the Americans reported the enemy fighters were in a loose formation and that the German pilots broke up to make their passes singly and in pairs, as a result of which two bombers were lost. The Mustang escort prevented the losses from being higher.

The Luftwaffe claims for nine heavy bombers by the jets do tally with American loss records, a figure which the USAAF reported 'compares favourably for the Germans with their other recent attempts to oppose the Eighth Air Force'. However, in addition to pilot and ground personnel losses, JG 7 had had 27 precious Me 262s destroyed that day, with a further eight damaged – a heavy blow from which it would prove very difficult to recover.

A *Geschwader Stabsstaffel* for JG 7 had been formed in late March following the disbandment of the semi-autonomous detachment known as *Kommando Stamp*, which had been unsuccessfully trialling air-to-air bombing methods with the Me 262. One of the *Kommando*'s pilots to be integrated into the *Stabsstaffel* was Leutnant Herbert Schlüter, who flew his first combat mission with JG 7 in mid-April led by Major Späte. Schlüter recalled:

We deployed five aircraft against a bomber formation that had attacked Dresden or Leipzig. My aircraft was armed with only two 30mm cannon and 24 R4M rockets. Shortly before we took off, a man ran over waving frantically and stepped up onto my wing. I opened the canopy and he shouted at me that I had a new version of the R4M rockets, and that I could fire from a distance of 1,000m. Once airborne, we soon had visual contact on the bombers – a formation of B-17s on a northwesterly heading. We climbed above the bombers and attacked from behind at a dive angle of three to five degrees and at high speed. At a distance of 900m, I had two tightly formated bombers in my sight and pushed the button to fire a salvo of rockets.

None of them fired! My first thought was perhaps corrosion under the button and I squeezed the button harder. Again, nothing happened. What I had not fully realised at the time was that my aircraft had sustained several hits from the defensive fire.

I decided to close in at high speed and pulled the throttle to idle. Unlike piston-engined aircraft, where the propeller acts as a brake and we could adjust our speed to that of the target, the Me 262 flew on without a noticeable reduction in speed. At a distance of about 200m, I fired the first burst. The rear of the Boeing – and particularly the stabiliser – was hit badly. Then I fired a burst into the left wing between the No 1 engine and the fuselage. Both engines were hit and the wing between the No 1 engine and the fuselage was ripped open. The wing was on fire, streaking flames. Many parts came away and sailed through the air. I kept firing and flew under the bomber at a distance of 10–20m.

A few seconds later, I felt a shudder in my aircraft as the left wing dipped, and at the same time the nose went down. After firing, I had gone back to full power immediately, and now I throttled back to idle and wanted to continue to fly in the horizontal position. I could not move the control column. With all my strength I tried again. Impossible! The control column would not budge. The angle of the wing increased and the air speed reached frightening levels. I had not looked at the air speed indicator even as I had approached the bombers. I knew from past experience that with a dive angle of five to seven degrees, a speed of 940km/h could be reached very quickly, and I was flying much faster than that now.

Leutnant Herbert Schlüter was involved in air-to-air bombing trials with the Me 262. They were unsuccessful, and he subsequently was assigned to the *Stabsstaffel* of JG 7, where he flew his first combat mission in a jet armed with R4M rockets. (EN Archive)

Many thoughts went through my head. I remembered from conversion training the insistent warnings of the instructors not to reach 1,000km/h. I had always followed that dictum. I had also thought about the experience of a fellow pilot who had reached, or gone beyond, the 1,000km/h limit. When he finally regained control, he had torn the fuel tank from its fixings and put a huge dent in the bottom of the fuselage.

Fortunately, at this point, the centrifugal forces ceased to be a problem. I was aware of the situation that I found myself in, and that I could not afford to make a mistake. The Me 262 had an electric aileron trim system. Very quickly, I tapped the trim toggle switch and, to my great relief, the left wing lifted a little. I repeated this several times and the wing lifted completely. Now I had to do the same thing to the elevator trim. This also worked. I was flying normally again. A little later, I set the trim to make the aircraft a little tail-heavy and it shot up rapidly. When the airspeed reached 860km/h, I grabbed the control column and the aircraft was under full control once more.

A few minutes later, I spotted a group of P-51 Mustangs – about 50 or 60 of them – 500m below me, flying in my direction! I just attacked immediately in a 12–15-degree dive. The Americans had obviously seen me, and they discarded their drop tanks and dived away!

Schlüter landed at Prague-Ruzyne, where he was startled to discover that his starboard wing had been hit with 12 bullets, both jet engines were damaged,

parts of the cowling had been torn away at high speed and the pods containing the fuel for the R4Ms had burned through but the rockets were still basically intact. He concluded that the Me 262 had been hit before he had attempted to fire the R4Ms.

Meanwhile, over southern Germany on 16 April, a formation of Me 262s – possibly as many as 14 – from JV 44 led by Generalleutnant Galland, with some aircraft equipped for the first time with R4M rockets, took off to intercept B-26 Marauders. The *Verbandsführer* claimed two bombers shot down, which corresponds with two losses suffered by the 322nd BG to enemy action that day.

On 20 April, as Adolf Hitler celebrated his birthday under a rain of American bombs in Berlin, JV 44 put up a formation of Me 262s during the late morning against B-26s of the 323rd BG targeting the marshalling yards at Memmingen. Just after 1100 hrs, and under clear blue skies, the Me 262s, some of which were carrying R4M rockets, climbed to attack the bombers from the east in loosely formated *Ketten* at 3,000–4,000m over the Kempten–Memmingen area. Unteroffizier Eduard Schallmoser, flying in the vanguard of the German force, readied himself for an attack. The bombers were maintaining a deliberately tight formation in order to maximise the density of their defensive fire and to prevent the jets from breaking up their individual elements.

As the first *Kette* closed in on the Marauders from 'six' and 'seven o'clock low', the tail gunners opened up, but the speed of the Messerschmitts combined with the fire from their 30mm weapons was devastating. A burst from an MK 108 shattered the port engine of B-26 41-31918 *Can't Get Started* of the 454th BS, flown by 1Lt Dale E. Sanders, which was already trailing black smoke, before an R4M rocket speared into the fuselage. Gunner TSgt Robert M Radlein in a neighbouring bomber watched in horror as the Me 262s came in to attack:

I looked out of the right waist window and right then this Me 262 appeared, right up alongside us, three o'clock level, about 100 yards out, effectively flying in formation with us. Instantly, I charged my gun and started firing. My gunnery training had taught me to fire short bursts of about ten rounds. I did it all automatically. I fired about five bursts of about ten rounds each at the Me 262 and I watched my tracers lag behind his tail, which probably meant that I was punching holes somewhere in his fuselage. He pulled away and left, but almost immediately another Me 262 pulled up into the same slot. I don't know what they had on their minds, but it was giving me good target practice, so I fired off about 20 rounds at the second Me 262 and then my gun jammed. I cleared the jam in two or three seconds, but by that time he was gone.

Looking out of his window again, Radlein saw Sanders' aircraft career across the sky, and the damage that the R4M had inflicted. He recalled:

Our top turret gunner, SSgt Edmundo Estrada, started firing. He had just raised his guns straight up and was shooting at an Me 262 passing overhead. He yelled,

'I got him! I got him!' because he had seen all kinds of metal and debris come flying past our aircraft. Estrada was convinced he had hit the jet, but unfortunately the pieces of metal he had seen had come not from the German fighter but from our No 3 aircraft piloted by Lt Sanders.

I looked out of my left waist window at Sanders' plane as it started to drop away from the main formation, and was able to see the entire radio compartment. The fighter attack had stripped away all the metal from the top of the wing, the radio man and navigator's compartment – I guess from just aft of the windows in the pilot's compartment – and, of course, one engine was also gone. I watched him falling out of formation and reached over to snap on my chest pack chute because things were warming up pretty fast.

In his Me 262 'White 11', Schallmoser had attempted to open fire on the B-26s, but his MK 108s jammed. Once again, as he had done on 4 April, Schallmoser quickly looked down at his gun firing button and, as

---

1300 hrs, 10 APRIL 1945

ORANIENBURG AIRFIELD

1 Some 1,232 B-17s and B-24s of the Eighth Air Force, with nearly 900 escort fighters, strike at German airfields and other facilities. The bomber stream splits up to attack different targets – the B-17s of the 3rd Air Division break up, with one stream heading for the JG 7 airfield at Brandenburg-Briest. Oberleutnant Walter Schuck leads a small formation of Me 262s of 3./JG 7 from Brandenburg-Briest to engage. He is flying 'Yellow 1'. The jets manoeuvre to attack the bombers from behind.

2 At a height of 8,000m, with a tight formation of Me 262s behind him, Schuck 'surf-rides' along the top of the bomber stream.

3 As bombs rain down on nearby Oranienburg, Schuck dives down from 1,000m above the B-17s and opens fire from 200m at a selected target. He then pulls up above the bomber, climbing back to 1,000m. The tail assembly of the B-17 breaks away and falls earthwards.

4 Schuck dives again, firing at and hitting B-17G 44-8427 *HENN'S REVENGE* of the 303rd BG between its two starboard engines. The stricken Flying Fortress lifts one wing and goes down.

5 With their ordnance dropped, the bombers turn east. Schuck spots a lone, badly damaged B-17 trailing smoke. As he circles it the crew bails out, so Schuck heads back to the main bomber stream without opening fire.

6 Schuck then shoots down a third bomber, punching a hole in its starboard wing.

7 Schuck claims his fourth victim, B-17G 43-38606 *Moonlight Mission* of the 457th BG, which again is hit between its two starboard engines. Debris flies away and a wing breaks off. Most of the crew bail out just before the bomber explodes at 5,000m.

8 As Schuck banks away, his Me 262 is fired upon by a P-51D Mustang flown by 1Lt Joseph Peterburs of the 55th FS/20th FG. The jet is hit in its port engine.

9 Schuck dives into cloud to escape, but the damaged turbojet engine begins to shed debris. At 1,200m he is forced to bail out. The Me 262 plunges earthward.

FOLLOWING PAGES

B-26G 44-68109 of the 455th BS/323rd BG, flown by 1Lt James H. Hansen, was lucky to make it back to its base at Denain-Prouvy, in France, following the JV 44 attack on 20 April 1945. The effects of Unteroffizier Eduard Schallmoser's close pass just beneath the Marauder's starboard engine are clearly visible on the propeller tips. (Author's Collection, courtesy of Moench)

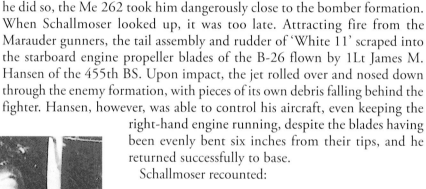

A remarkable photograph taken shortly after Unteroffizier Eduard Schallmoser bailed out of his Me 262 and landed by parachute in his mother's garden after avoiding a catastrophic collision with 1Lt James H. Hansen's B-26 over Bavaria on 20 April 1945. (Author's collection, courtesy of Schallmoser)

he did so, the Me 262 took him dangerously close to the bomber formation. When Schallmoser looked up, it was too late. Attracting fire from the Marauder gunners, the tail assembly and rudder of 'White 11' scraped into the starboard engine propeller blades of the B-26 flown by 1Lt James M. Hansen of the 455th BS. Upon impact, the jet rolled over and nosed down through the enemy formation, with pieces of its own debris falling behind the fighter. Hansen, however, was able to control his aircraft, even keeping the right-hand engine running, despite the blades having been evenly bent six inches from their tips, and he returned successfully to base.

Schallmoser recounted:

Basically, I turned too late and rammed the Marauder, which then fell away. Meanwhile, I knew my 'White 11' was a complete loss, and with my last reserves of strength I was able to escape the aircraft by parachute.

Remarkably good fortune would remain with Schallmoser, for having bailed out of his aircraft, he came down in his mother's garden in the small town of Lenzfried-im-Allgau! Folding up his parachute and suffering from a painful blow to one of his knees from when he left his aircraft, he limped into the family home, where his bewildered mother fed him with a plate of pancakes.

Meanwhile, Unteroffizier Johann-Karl Müller of JV 44 fired his R4M rockets towards the Marauders, and two of the bombers were hit. One rocket fired from the Me 262s struck B-26 42-96256 *Ugly Duckling*, whose pilot, 1Lt James L. Vining of the 455th BS, recalled:

In a fast glance over my shoulder, I saw a jet coming in out of a slight turn with muzzle flashes around the four 30mm cannon in the nose. I turned my attention back to my position, tucking my wing closer to No. 4, and at that instant a terrific blast went off below my knees and the plane rolled to the right. Sensing that my right leg was gone, I looked toward my co-pilot, and while ordering him to take his controls, I noted that the right engine was at idle speed. So, in one swift arcing motion with my right hand, I hit the feathering button, moved

---

1100 hrs, 20 APRIL 1945

MEMMINGEN

1 B-26 Marauders of the 323rd, 394th and 397th BGs are despatched to bomb the marshalling yard at Memmingen, in southern Germany.

2 JV 44 send up around 15 Me 262s from Munich-Riem in *Kette* formations to intercept the Marauders. The jets reach the B-26s between Kempten and Memmingen just after 1100 hrs. The lead *Kette* approaches the bombers from behind at high speed and open fire with their MK 108 cannon at close range.

3 One B-26 is quickly damaged and the bomber gunners simultaneously open fire at their attackers as they pass through the formation in alarming proximity.

4 Flying Me 262 'White 11', Unteroffizier Eduard Schallmoser attempts to fire his cannon, but they jam as he passes very close between two B-26s immediately above and below him.

5 Momentarily distracted by his jammed cannon, Schallmoser is unable to avoid catching the propeller blades of the B-26 just above him flown by 1Lt James M. Hansen of the 455th BS/323rd BG. Schallmoser's rudder is damaged in the process.

6 As Schallmoser fights to keep his Me 262 under control, more jets race in, attacking the lower boxes of B-26s.

7 Schallmoser's aircraft veers off to the right.

8 Schallmoser then turns towards the American formation again, but the jet attracts defensive fire from the bombers.

9 Schallmoser flies straight across the path of B-26F 42-96256 *Ugly Duckling*, flown by 1Lt James L. Vining of the 455th BS. Vining opens fire at the Me 262 with his four fixed forward-firing machine guns, as do the turret gunners in other B-26s in the formation. Debris starts to fall away from the Me 262 and it plumes smoke.

10 Meanwhile, Unteroffizier Johann-Karl Müller, flying Me 262 'White 15' of JV 44, fires his battery of R4M rockets into the rear of the bomber formation. Two of the rockets hit home, one striking *Ugly Duckling*. The rocket rips through the Marauder's fuselage, inflicting severe damage to the aircraft and wounding its crew.

11 Seconds later, Müller and the other Me 262s pull away.

12 With his Me 262 mortally damaged and diving for the ground, Schallmoser, with his 'last reserves of strength', bails out.

FOLLOWING PAGES

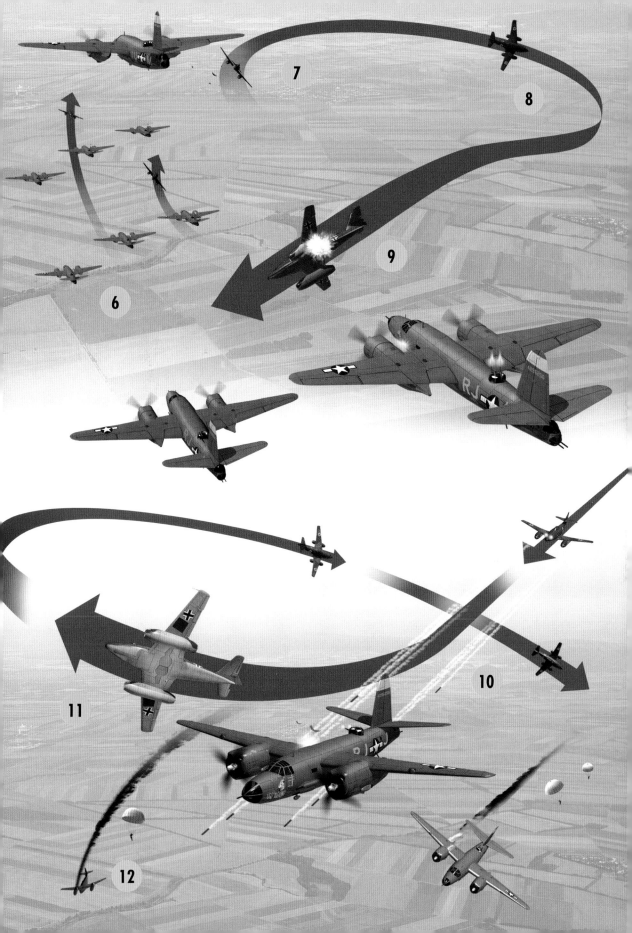

A remarkable air-to-air photograph taken from the waist position of a Marauder of the 323rd BG on 20 April 1945 as an Me 262 of JV 44 passes through the flight of bombers seen at the base of the photograph and flying below 44-68132 of the 456th BS. The jet is visible as the small light-coloured aircraft passing just behind the rearmost B-26 at the right of the flight. Another Marauder in the rear flight, visible immediately below 44-68132, appears to have been hit and is on fire, possibly as a result of being attacked by the jet. (Author's Collection, courtesy of Moench)

to the overhead rudder trim crank and trimmed the plane for single engine operation and, just as rapidly, pressed the intercom button to order the bombardier to jettison the two tons of bombs. We were losing altitude at 2,000ft per minute, which slowed to 1,000ft per minute with the load gone.

As Vining's B-26 fell away from its formation, the relatively inexperienced co-pilot took control of the aircraft and the radio operator/navigator applied a tourniquet to Vining's shattered leg. He also gave the gravely wounded pilot some morphine. Meanwhile, the lone 'straggler' began to attract more attacks from the jets, which attempted to finish it off. Miraculously, despite the substantial damage inflicted by the R4M, the Marauder remained airborne. Although subsequently attacked by Me 262s of I./KG(J) 54, the B-26 managed to return to friendly territory, where it crash-landed on an abandoned airfield close to the French border.

By the time JV 44's Me 262s had turned away from the 323rd BG, they had shot down three B-26s and damaged a further seven. No German pilots were reported lost, but Schallmoser's aircraft was destroyed, and it is likely several others had been damaged during the attack.

USAAF tactical air forces again mounted large-scale operations against targets across southern Germany on 24 April. During the afternoon American aircraft struck at a range of airfields, transport targets, oil storage and supply depots north of Munich. A force of 256 medium bombers was sent out, including 74 B-26s of the 322nd and 344th BGs, detailed to strike at an oil depot hidden in woods near Schrobenhausen, 50km northwest of Munich. It was supplying fuel to German troops heading into the so-called Alpine 'Redoubt' area, from where it was intended they would launch a last stand against the approaching Allies.

Oberst Günther Lützow led a force of six Me 262s to intercept. As the ringleader of what he perceived to have been a 'mutiny', an affronted Göring had assigned Lützow, a holder of the Knight's Cross with Oakleaves, a former *Kommodore* of JG 3 and only the second German fighter pilot to be credited with 100 victories, to Galland's *Jagdverband* of renegades. For this mission Lützow was joined by fellow Knight's Cross-holders Hauptmann Walter Krupinski and Oberleutnant Klaus Neumann. The jets took off to the northwest, but two were forced to abort early due to mechanical problems. The remaining four, of which at least Lützow's and Neumann's aircraft were carrying R4Ms, swept across the Jura mountains to take on the bombers.

Lützow had already been in the air that morning when he led 11 Me 262s armed with R4Ms to engage B-26s of the 17th BG tasked with bombing Schwabmünchen, south of Augsburg. On that mission at least two bombers had been shot down.

Just before 1530 hrs, as the last B-26s from the 344th BG were setting up to make their bomb run, the jets broke through cloud and attacked the Marauders' 'window' chaff flight from high and low southeast of Monheim at a height of 7,000m, diving to just under 3,500m. The crew of the B-26C of 2Lt R. M. Cello of the 495th BS flying the No. 1 position of the 'window' flight reported that the Me 262s:

> . . . made their first pass from low at 7 o'clock under the aircraft and broke at 2 o'clock level, turned and came from low at 1 o'clock, closed to 200 yards then fired to within 20 yards. One Me 262 came from pursuit curve and tail gunner opened fire at 600 yards. Gun jammed but fighter broke off at 500 yards.

1Lt E. L. Johnson, at the controls of the neighbouring Marauder, also observed how the jets came in from 'seven o'clock below' and passed under the bombers, breaking away at 'two' or 'three o'clock', but did not fire on that pass. Instead, confirming the Cello crew account, they then returned from low at 'one o'clock' and closed to 50 yards, firing as they neared, before breaking away at 'seven o'clock low' and diving into cloud.

2Lt William P. Morton was flying a B-26 of the 494th BS:

> I was in the No. 6 position, third flight. Near the target, I was fully absorbed in keeping tight formation. But I recall that the intercom conversation was warning that some strange-looking fighters were firing cannon at us. According to my gunners they were well out of range of our 0.50-cal. guns. Then I caught a glimpse of this object out of my left eye and it was moving like a bat out of hell.

Sgt Jonny Quong was the top turret gunner on board Morton's aircraft:

> I saw what seemed at first to be a twin-engined B-26 straggler at long distance approaching at six o'clock. As it kept approaching, all the gunners saw it. It kept

---

COLLISION

On 20 April 1945, 15 Me 262s of JV 44 carried out an attack on B-26s of the 323rd BG over Bavaria. The jets flew in three-aircraft *Kette* formations and attacked the bombers from behind. Some of the Me 262s carried R4M 55mm rockets under their wings. This artwork depicts the moment that Unteroffizier Eduard Schallmoser, flying Me 262A-1a 'White 11', distracted by checking his firing button, passed almost fatally close to the starboard engine of B-26G 44-68109, flown by 1Lt James M. Hansen of the 455th BS. In doing so, Schallmoser's Me 262 clipped six inches from the Marauder's propeller blades and sheared the tip of the jet's tail assembly. Attracting fire from the other B-26s in the formation, the Me 262 dived through the bombers with pieces of its own debris falling behind it. While Schallmoser was forced to bail out, Hansen and his crew returned safely to base.

coming and then dived and broke off to the left. When it turned, I could tell it was not a B-26 but a smaller plane going like a bat out of hell. All the gunners started talking excitedly. 'What the hell was that?' We were so excited that our pilot had to tell us to keep quiet.

Neumann immediately fired his R4M rockets and thought he observed two Marauders break out of formation, while Krupinski saw another B-26 trailing black smoke but managing to remain with the group. Then, almost as fast as the jets had come, they were gone, arcing in a wide turn to port below the bombers and heading towards the cloud in a loose formation. At that moment it seems that the P-47s of the 365th FG assigned as escort that day fell past the bombers in pursuit of the jets. 2Lt James L. Stalter, flying B-26 43-34181 *Lak-a-Nookie* of the 344th BG, remembered:

We were heading for home when I heard our Group Leader call the leader of our P-47 escort, stating 'We have visitors'. The fighter leader's response still sticks in my mind. In a very, very slow, southern Texas drawl, he responded, 'Okay, we'll be right down'.

Flying a P-47 that day was 1Lt Oliven T. Cowan, leading 'Green Flight', who spotted the Me 262s climbing up to attack the 365th's charges. He flipped his fighter over and rolled it into a sharp dive, just fast enough to catch the jets as they swept through the bombers seconds after firing their rockets:

I recall thinking that my dive needed more speed, and I became more aware of this as the jets pulled away. At this point, I suddenly realised that I was talking out loud to my plane to give more speed, and then I wondered how much of this was on the radio. We had no fear of the German jets, because we could easily out-turn them. I am sure they had no fear of us, because usually they could leave us. Hence, we needed altitude for speed (diving) and a surprise element. But with the jet's speed, they could hit fast and move on.

Leading the 365th's 'Blue Flight' was Capt Jerry G. Mast:

I was about 2,000ft above the last element in the first box when the 262, one of a flight of four which had been broken up by 'Green Flight', started to make an attack from 6 o'clock low on the box of B-26s which I was covering. I split-S'd and went into a full power dive to cut the 262 off from the bombers. The pilot of the 262 saw me, for he went into a steep dive before he had the opportunity to fire on the bombers.

Mast's wingman, 2Lt Byron Smith Jr, flying as 'Blue 2', had followed his leader in his dive on the Me 262:

I observed one Me 262 flying parallel and to the right of the B-26s. 'Blue Leader' and I gave chase in an attempt to cut the enemy plane off from the bombers. I was able to close slightly as the Me 262 made a left turn in front of the bombers. He then made a steep right turn into the bombers. I pulled lead and fired a burst over his nose. The jet continued his turn when he saw me and made a series of violent turns, climbs and glides. I was able to fire several bursts at him and observe my tracers go into his ship before he finally dove under the clouds. I was forced to return to my squadron and continue the escort.

Smith claimed the jet as a 'damaged.'

Meanwhile, Mast and 2Lt William H. Myers, flying as 'Red 2', noticed that the Me 262 they were pursuing jointly at a speed of more than 500mph had started to pull out from its dive, but then suddenly went into an even steeper dive, its pilot having probably become aware of the two American fighters following him. The jet 'went into the ground and exploded', and

1530 hrs, 24 APRIL 1945

MONHEIM

1 A force of 74 B-26 Marauders of the 322nd and 344th BGs are detailed to bomb an oil depot in woods near Schrobenhausen, 50km northwest of Munich, under escort from P-47s.

2 Oberst Günther Lützow of JV 44 leads six Me 262s up from Munich-Riem to intercept the B-26s, but two jets have to abort. Lützow and the three remaining fighters fly on and catch the Marauders southeast of Monheim at a height of 7,000m, approaching from behind and out of cloud.

3 The Me 262s are spotted by 1Lt Oliven T. Cowan, leading 'Green Flight' of the escorting 388th FS/365th FG. Cowan dives down sharply, attempting to engage the jets as they pass out of the bomber formation after firing their 30mm cannon and R4M rockets. He manages to hit one of the Me 262s.

4 Bounced by the P-47s, the Me 262s break up and scatter, diving away.

5 One of the jets, probably flown by Lützow, breaks left and endeavours to re-approach the bombers in a dive.

6 This Me 262 is then observed heading south by Capt Jerry G. Mast, who is leading the 388th FS's 'Blue Flight'. Accompanied by 2Lt William H. Myers, the two P-47 pilots pursue the fleeing jet in a power dive.

7 In the meantime, Mast's wingman, 2Lt Byron Smith Jr, chases another Me 262.

8 This jet makes a series of violent turns before climbing through the bombers to evade the Thunderbolt.

9 Smith fires several bursts, and although he strikes the Me 262, the jet escapes through cloud.

10 Mast and Myers, meanwhile, are now diving at more than 500mph in pursuit of 'their' jet.

11 Lützow, still diving towards the south, but very sharply now, is unable to evade the P-47s.

12 Lützow's Me 262 crashes into the ground on the outskirts of Donauwörth, between Ulm and Ingolstadt. It was the only aircraft of this type reported as lost by the Luftwaffe that day. Lützow is killed.

13 Mast and Myers break away violently, with the latter briefly blacking out when he has to pull his P-47 into a high-G turn to port in order to avoid hitting the ground himself.

Oberst Günther Lützow (left) and Oberst Johannes Steinhoff prepare for a daily briefing outside the wooden hut which JV 44 occupied as its dispersal at Munich-Riem. Steinhoff recorded that this area 'was a masterpiece of improvisation, consisting basically of a table and a few rickety chairs set up in the middle of a patch of weeds and undergrowth'. Note the motorcycle used as a form of transport around the airfield. Steinhoff and Lützow effectively held operational command of JV 44 during the first half of April 1945. (Author's Collection)

Myers was forced to black himself out with a high-G recovery in order to avoid hitting the ground himself.

For the JV 44 pilots this was a critical moment. The jet chased by Mast and Myers was flying furthest to the south of the German group. This was Lützow's aircraft. Radio contact had apparently been lost between Lützow and the other jets, and he was observed by Krupinski to turn quite suddenly and inexplicably towards the south. Moments later, as Lützow flew away alone from the formation towards the mountains, Krupinski witnessed:

. . . an explosion in the air. We broke away in a wide left turn on our homeward route. Lützow's change in course towards the south was completely incomprehensible to me, and I therefore called him on the radio but did not get a reply. The explosion which I saw, or something very similar, occurred at a distance of at least 20km. Everyone knows that at that distance, details cannot be observed. In any case, my attempt at radio contact, prompted by Lützow's change in course, took place before I saw the explosion. We couldn't fly after him, as contact with the enemy Marauders had taken place quite late into the mission and we were compelled to fly home by the quickest route due to lack of fuel.

The three remaining Me 262s landed back at Riem and their pilots reported three 'probable' claims over B-26s, although the Americans reported no aircraft missing. Lützow did not return, and it is believed that his Me 262 had crashed into some waste ground in the town of Donauwörth, between Ulm and Ingolstadt. It was the only aircraft of this type reported as lost by the Luftwaffe that day.

Commenting after the war, Johannes Steinhoff was of the opinion that being unfamiliar with the Me 262, Lützow was 'nervous' about flying it, especially since he had not flown combat missions for some time. For the pilots and groundcrew of JV 44, the loss of such a respected and experienced unit commander and staff officer was a severe blow.

But as the war turned inexorably against Nazi Germany, Lützow's loss was just one of many. The Luftwaffe simply did not have enough pilots or aircraft to strike back at the Allies' air power. Symbolically, on 26 April, Galland's jet was shot up. At 1130 hrs he took off from Riem leading a formation of 12 Me 262s from JV 44 all carrying R4Ms to engage B-26s from the 17th BG that were targeting the recently evacuated jet base at Lechfeld and the ammunition dump at Schrobenhausen. Although five Marauders were claimed shot down, Galland made an error as he approached the bombers when he forgot to flick off the second safety switch for the rockets, probably as a result of the distraction of defensive fire. As his jet progressed among the bombers, it was hit by machine gun fire and began to trail smoke.

1Lt James J. Finnegan (left) of the 10th FS/50th FG and his crew chief sit on the nose of their P-47D *The Irish Shillalah*. Finnegan opened fire on the Me 262 of Generalleutnant Adolf Galland on 26 April 1945, and is credited with inflicting sufficient damage on the German ace's jet to force it down. Finnegan recalled that he 'had never seen anything move that fast'. (Author's Collection, courtesy of Finnegan)

Shortly after midday, P-47s of the 27th and 50th FGs came to the aid of the Marauders, diving down from a higher altitude and firing their machine guns as they gave chase to the quickly dispersing jets. Leading 'Green Flight' of the 10th FS/50th FG was 1Lt James J. Finnegan. He recalled:

I remember it well because it was the first time I saw operational jets. We had been briefed on them because they had been expected and used since October 1944. Yet, like a lot of intelligence we received in those times, nothing ever materialised.

Finnegan was about to have a rude shock. Seconds earlier he had watched in astonishment as two 'darts' streaked through the bomber formation just as two Marauders exploded in flames, at which point the 'darts' broke away to the left and right, respectively. 'Somebody yelled "Jet Bandits!" over the intercom', Finnegan remembered. 'There was no doubt in my mind what they were; I had never seen anything move that fast'. He then spotted what appeared to be a damaged Messerschmitt:

I kept the 'bandit' that turned left in my sight and watched the bombers from my 11 o'clock position. I told my Flight I was going down after him, turned on my back in a split-S manoeuvre and caught him in my gunsight. Although the Me 262 was a great deal faster than the Thunderbolt, nothing could out-dive it, and I had the advantage of height. I pulled the big nose up so it obscured the jet, held the trigger for about a 1½–2-second burst, dropped the nose and saw strikes on the right wing root. The ship pulled abruptly left and disappeared in the clouds. I claimed an Me 262 as 'damaged and probable' and thought no more of it.

Galland described how:

A hail of fire enveloped me. A sharp rap hit my right knee, the instrument panel with its indispensable instruments was shattered, the right engine was also hit –

Vulnerable moments – an Me 262 is pursued at low level by an American fighter as the jet makes its landing approach with gear down. This was the time when, with its speed reduced, the Me 262 became prey to fighter attack. The Americans dubbed such attacks 'rat-catching'. (EN Archive)

its metal covering worked loose in the wind and was partly carried away – and now the left engine was hit. I could hardly hold her in the air.

I had only one wish: to get out of this 'crate' which now apparently was only good for dying in. But then I was paralysed by the terror of being shot while parachuting down. Experience had taught us that we jet fighter pilots had to reckon on this. I soon discovered that after some adjustments my battered Me 262 could be steered again and, after a dive through the layer of cloud, I saw the Autobahn below me. Ahead lay Munich and to the left, Riem. In a few seconds I was over the airfield. Having regained my self-confidence, I gave the customary wing wobble and started banking to come in. It was remarkably quiet and dead below. One engine did not react at all to the throttle, and as I could not reduce it, I had to cut both engines just before the edge of the airfield. A long trail of smoke drifted behind me.

The Me 262 bumped to a halt with a flat tyre as Galland threw open the canopy and clambered out awkwardly, just as Allied fighter-bombers had begun a strafing run over Riem. He was about to fall into the 'shelter' of a bomb crater when he was welcomed by a timely mechanic riding a semi-tracked *Kettenkrad* tow vehicle. The Generalleutnant limped gratefully over to it and the little vehicle rumbled off to safety with Galland trembling and shocked on the rear seat. It was, effectively, the end of his war, and JV 44 had only a few days of operations left.

The next day (27 April), nearly 600km away to the northeast, some of JG 7's Me 262s undertook a ground-attack mission against enemy supply columns near Cottbus and, along with aircraft from III./KG(J) 6 and I./KG(J) 54, destroyed 65 vehicles. On the way home, however, the jet fighters ran into some Soviet Il-2s. Despite being low on fuel and ammunition, a few of the

Me 262s took on the fearsome Soviet *Shturmoviks*. Leutnant Herbert Schlüter recalls a mission around this time:

I flew only a very few missions. I never found out the reason for this. I assume it was the lack of fuel and spare parts, as well as the fact that we had more pilots than aircraft. I did, however, fly three missions over the Eastern Front. The orders were to attack Russian troops on the ground. Our aircraft were armed with two MK 108 cannon for this task, and on one occasion a 250kg bomb was slung under the fuselage. I always flew alone, but did not see much action either because there were no enemy troops in the target area or because I was unable to distinguish between friendly and enemy troops.

On one of these flights, as I was returning to Prague-Ruyzne, I encountered an enemy fighter-bomber formation flying on a southwesterly heading at an altitude between 1,800–2,000m. There was a large number of Il-2s in rows of eight to ten, with more flying on a parallel course behind them. Numerous fighters escorted the formation above and below.

I attacked the formation but the fighters saw me and turned to attack. I could not chance a dogfight. I turned and made off towards the east, only to turn again and renew my attack. Again the fighters spotted me and I had to break off. It became clear that only the element of surprise would promise success. After flying to the east once more, I turned and flew at an altitude of 180–200m on a southwesterly heading. When I saw the formation above, I pulled up with full power and found a number of fighters in front of me. I was very close when they turned to attack me. Now, with reduced speed, I was able to pull tighter turns. A burst of fire and a fighter exploded. I was almost hit by the debris. I was suddenly in the middle of the formation, and since I could not risk a dogfight, I had to break away again.

The Me 262 had lost airspeed and accelerated slower than a conventional aircraft, so I decided to play an old trick familiar to fighter pilots of all nations when it was imperative to stick to an opponent who was trying to evade by out-turning his pursuer – deflection shooting. Well – I was the pursued, and I had to counter their attempt to hit me. I 'dropped' my left wing in order to fake a turn, held the rudder down and flew straight at a declining angle of 12 to 15 degrees at full power as salvos of large-calibre bright red tracer streamed by my left side. The Russians had learned their lessons well. Despite the seriousness of the situation, I could not help but have a little laugh. My fuel was too low for another attack. We needed a fuel reserve because of the Mustangs, whose practice it was to wait for us at Prague-Ruyzne. My 'kill' was a probable because I did not have a witness and I did not observe the wreckage hit the ground.

It is believed that JG 7 accounted for approximately 20 Soviet aircraft destroyed during the last weeks of the war, but in the period 28 April to 1 May, the *Geschwader* lost some ten jets.

There is no doubt the Me 262 introduced a new dimension into the air war over Europe, and one that did shock the Allies through its speed and armament. But there were never enough of them, and for all the revolutionary design, sophistication and engineering, the Me 262 was simply beaten by a greater strength of force.

AFTERMATH

Hardly had the guns fallen silent in May 1945 than liberated Europe was chilled by a 'Cold War'. Despite a costly conflict, the pace of military and technological advancement became a race between the victors, some of whom emerged as 'superpowers'. One vital element in the scramble for strategic dominance in this new global climate was the continued development of the jet engine and the refinement of aeronautical innovations such as the swept wing, the origins of which lay in the years of the 'hot' war. In this, the Me 262, despite its undoubted but all too brief impact on the course of the air war in 1944–45, played a key role.

The United States had already flown its first jet aircraft, the Bell XP-59A Airacomet, in October 1942, but it was soon superseded by the Lockheed P-80 Shooting Star, which, as the F-80, saw service during the early stages of the Korean War, where it performed well against ageing Soviet piston-engined Yak-9s and Il-10s. However, the straight-winged F-80 would be more than matched by the appearance of the superlative Soviet MiG-15 single-engined jet fighter with its swept-back wing. The latter was inspired to some extent by Hans Multhopp's wartime design of the Focke-Wulf Ta 183. It was also similar to the swept wings of the Me 262 and Messerschmitt's later P.1101 single-jet project design.

In Korean skies, Soviet and Chinese pilots initially gave a good account of themselves in the MiG-15, which proved to be well suited to combat conditions. Indeed, the fighter was a potent adversary for United Nations' aircraft during the encounters that took place over 'MiG Alley', as the China–North Korea border area around the Yalu River became known.

However, from December 1950, the MiG-15 would be pitted against the USAF's equally superlative North American Aviation (NAA) F-86 Sabre. Although built with a single General Electric jet engine as opposed to the twin Jumo 004 units used by the Me 262, the aircraft bore a marked similarity to the Messerschmitt in plan view thanks to its moderate 35-degree swept-back wing. The latter had first been proposed in a design by NAA from September 1945 – just five months after the end of World War II, and thus influenced by German design. It also featured an all-round vision, teardrop-shaped bubble canopy akin to and probably influenced by that of the Me 262. In Korea, the MiG-15 and the F-86 fought each other for air superiority for two-and-a-half years.

The USAF also deployed B-29 Superfortress bombers to Korea between 1950–53, and these were initially involved in daylight missions. In a repeat of the action over Europe in 1944–45, when a handful of Me 262s battled against USAAF B-17s and B-24s, and their escorts, the relatively small numbers of MiG-15s attempted to shoot the B-29s down. These aircraft enjoyed some early successes, as the F-80 and F-84 Thunderjet escorts proved unable to defend the B-29s. Only the urgent deployment of 50 F-86s of the 4th Fighter Wing partially neutralised the threat. The USAF had some 30 B-29s shot down or badly damaged by MiG-15s, forcing the Superfortress units to switch exclusively to night attacks. In essence, the campaign waged by the MiG-15s against the B-29s was a repeat of the B-17/B-24 –Me 262–P-51 scenario of 1944–45.

The design of the Me 262, its propulsion system, its integrated cannon and underwing rocket armament went on to influence both late-war German projects as well as American and Soviet jet fighter aircraft well into the 1950s and beyond.